PRAISE FOR *FAMILY SHIFT*

Today's families need hope and direction now more than ever and that is why I am excited about *Family Shift*. My friends Rodney and Michelle Gage have put together a simple 5-Step Plan that will help you define your vision for your marriage and family relationships. I am excited to join the movement of helping families stop drifting and start living with greater intention.

—TobyMac
Grammy Award Winning Recording Artist

We are so excited about *Family Shift*! Even though we are just getting started in the marriage and parenting season of our lives, we need all the help we can get to continue building upon the foundation our parents laid for us. We love how Rodney and Michelle help couples and families clearly define how to write their own mission and vision statements and how to identify their own core values as a couple and family. This book truly serves as a spiritual and moral compass to help families successfully navigate through life in today's world.

—John Luke and Mary Kate Robertson
Duck Dynasty Stars

For over three decades, I have coached young people on how to win on and off the field. If there is one thing a team must have in order to win a ball game, it is a successful game plan. However, even a successful game plan still requires making adjustments. In *Family Shift*, Rodney and Michelle Gage not only provide a solid game plan but also help you know how to make the necessary adjustments along the way in your most important relationships. The book can be a game changer for your marriage and family.

—Coach Lou Holtz
Legendary Football Coach

If there was ever a time for families to make a shift to reclaim the eroding spiritual and moral values of our culture it is now. Rodney and Michelle Gage have provided a simple yet powerful framework on how to make the necessary shifts to keep their family from drifting further away from God and each other. I highly recommend this book!

—Josh McDowell
Bestselling Author and Speaker

After having won five World Series in my career, I know it requires special chemistry and teamwork to have a championship team. The same is true when it comes to the family. As a husband and father of four kids, I know it requires having special chemistry and teamwork to overcome the curve balls and changeups our culture is constantly pitching at us. This book provides families with a proven plan to help couples and parents achieve winning families.

—**Andy Pettitte**
Five-Time World Series Champion and Three-Time All-Star

If marriages or families are going to avoid being negatively influenced in today's culture they have to have a plan to follow. *Family Shift* provides a proven plan and framework that will keep your marriage and family relationships focused on what matters most. If you want to avoid drifting apart, this book is a must-read.

—**David and Jason Benham**
Bestselling Authors, Nationally Acclaimed Entrepreneurs,
and Speakers

We all want a loving family environment where each person—parent and child—experiences life in all the fullness that Jesus talked about. What Rodney and Michelle have done in their timely book *Family Shift* is provide a clear and intentional path for parents to create a life-giving environment where children can flourish to their greatest potential. Through my work at Compassion, I've witnessed the impact of the holistic strategies included in *Family Shift* to transform lives for the good—one family at a time—all over the world. In a world where so many forces are working against having a healthy family life, this book is a gift to any parent who wants the best for their children!

—**Santiago "Jimmy" Mellado**
President and CEO of Compassion International

Having known Rodney, Michelle, and their whole family for years, we are excited that they have written *Family Shift* to share their own proven method of seeing God's plan fulfilled in marriage and family relationships. It is our hope that this book will encourage and strengthen other families just as it has our own.

—**Jerry and Becki Falwell**
President and of Liberty University

Strong marriages and raising powerful kids who know who they are don't just happen. It takes a lot of prayer, patience, wisdom, and intentionality to keep from drifting toward the norms of our culture. This is why I am so excited about *Family Shift*. I have seen firsthand how Rodney and Michelle live out the principles of this book in their own marriage and family. They have given us a much-needed framework along with practical tools we can all apply to help safeguard our most important relationships.

—Andi Andrew
Co-Pastor of Liberty Church, Speaker, and Author of
She Is Free **and** *Fake or Follower*

Success can be defined as being loved and respected by those who know you the best. No one knows us better than those living under our own roof. In *Family Shift*, my friends Rodney and Michelle Gage identify 5 critical shifts to help families experience true success in their most important relationships. I highly recommend this book to couples and parents seeking to live with greater purpose and intention.

—Shawn Lovejoy
Author and President and CEO of Courage To Lead

A strong family is not built on chance, but on making the right choices. That is why *Family Shift* is such a timely book. Our friends Rodney and Michelle outline five important shifts every couple can make to help redirect their lives and transform their most important relationships, bringing life to families.

—Pastor Ed and Lisa Young
Senior Pastor at Fellowship Church, Grapevine, Texas, and
New York Times **Bestselling Authors**

We know firsthand how demanding careers can pull our focus away from the ones we love most. With so much of modern culture competing for our attention, it's no wonder marriages and children drift apart. In their new book, *Family Shift* Rodney and Michelle Gage layout a clear 5-Step Plan for keeping our priorities in line. They show us how being intentional about our relationships is the best way to stop "the drift" and cement those precious family bonds.

—David and Nicole Crank
Senior Pastors of Faith Church, St. Louis, MO and
West Palm Beach, FL

Having a successful marriage and raising morally strong kids doesn't just happen in today's world—you have to be intentional. Even more, you need a plan. Rodney and Michelle Gage have given families a step-by-step approach to achieving healthy homes and strong family relationships. Whether you're thinking about marriage, already have kids, or live in a blended family situation, *Family Shift* will give you the help and show you how to live with greater intention as a family.

—Dr. Jack Graham
Senior Pastor of Prestonwood Baptist Church, Dallas, Texas

I have known Rodney and Michelle Gage for years and have watched their children develop into amazing leaders. The principles and proven framework they offer in *Family Shift* is exactly what today's families need to avoid being swept away in the cultural currents that are destroying so many families. *Family Shift* will give you the hope, direction, and encouragement you need to reach your family's full potential. I highly recommend this book to anyone ready to make the necessary shifts to start living with greater intention.

—Layne Schranz
Associate Pastor of Church of the Highlands and
Pikes Peak Hill Climb Racing Champion

Just as the keys to creating a great dish are using good ingredients and following a proven recipe, having a solid marriage and strong family is no different. Rodney and Michelle provide couples and parents a tried and tested recipe for success in *Family Shift* that is easy to follow and guaranteed to transform your house into a home the way God intended.

—John Rivers
Chef and Owner of 4 Rivers Smokehouse

Having a successful marriage and family takes work, commitment, sacrifice, and, most of all, a lot of love and forgiveness toward each other. In their book, *Family Shift* my friends Rodney and Michelle share five critical steps that will help your family move from where you are to where you desire to be.

—Dr. Dave Martin
Bestselling Author, Speaker, and Success Coach

Living with intentionality is easier said than done. However, it's the only way families can not only survive but thrive in today's world. *Family Shift* provides the much-needed tools and is the how-to guide to keep your families on track in the things that matter most in your life. We highly recommend this book!

—Bil and Jessica Cornelius
Pastors of Church Unlimited, Corpus Christi, Texas

FAMILY
SHIFT

FAMILY
SHIFT

*The 5-Step Plan to Stop Drifting and
Start Living with Greater Intention*

RODNEY & MICHELLE GAGE

WORTHY®

New York • Nashville

Worthy
Hachette Book Group
1290 Avenue of the Americas, New York, NY 10104
worthypublishing.com
twitter.com/worthypub

First Edition: September 2019

Worthy is a division of Hachette Book Group, Inc. The Worthy name and logo are trademarks of Hachette Book Group, Inc.

The publisher is not responsible for websites (or their content) that are not owned by the publisher.

The Hachette Speakers Bureau provides a wide range of authors for speaking events. To find out more, go to www.hachettespeakersbureau.com or call (866) 376-6591.

Cover design by Michael J. Williams.
Print book interior design by Bart Dawson. Interior art: shutterstock.com

Library of Congress Control Number: 2019946334

ISBNs: 978-1-5460-1466-9 (hardcover); 978-1-5460-1465-2 (ebook)

Printed in the United States of America
LSC-C
10 9 8 7 6 5 4 3 2 1

This book resulted from the incredible legacy of faith that our parents, Freddie and Barbara Gage and Rod and Linda Masteller, have shared with us through their love for God and each other. Our lives and the lives of our three children are fruit from the seeds they have sown.

CONTENTS

Introduction: Notice the Drift   1

STEP 1: START WITH THE END IN MIND

1. On Your Mark   9
2. Get Set   25
3. Go!   41

STEP 2: HOLD TO CORE VALUES

4. Family Is a Team Sport   57
5. Rule Books, Playbooks, and the Good Book   73
6. What Gets Rewarded Gets Repeated   87

STEP 3: IDENTIFY YOUR GPS

7. Envision the Future   103
8. Do What Comes Naturally   121
9. Toughen Up   137

STEP 4: FIND LIFE-GIVING FRIENDSHIPS

10. Iron Sharpens Iron   153
11. Every Friendship Needs a Little TLC   169

STEP 5: TEACH BY EXAMPLE

12. Who's on Point?   185
13. The Power of Unconditional Love   201
14. Leaving the Nest   217

Acknowledgments   231
Notes   233

INTRODUCTION

NOTICE THE DRIFT

Every family ends up somewhere, but few families end up somewhere on purpose.

Years ago we (Rodney and Michelle) went on a trip to Cancún, Mexico, with Michelle's three sisters, their husbands, and Michelle's mom and dad. While there, one of our most memorable activities was snorkeling. The experience began with us riding WaveRunners through the lagoon's mangrove canals and into the ocean. Our tour guide rode out ahead, leading us to an amazing Caribbean coral reef. Just before we jumped off our watercrafts into the water, he reminded us to adhere to the "check in or check out" rule, which encourages snorkelers to come up to the surface, look around, and "check in" about every ten to fifteen minutes. He wanted us to be aware of our location at all times, because the undercurrent could cause us to drift out to sea.

All of us jumped in, put our faces down, and immediately were amazed by the incredible beauty of the underwater world. We explored a beautiful coral reef containing all kinds of colorful fish and unusual creatures. We were so engrossed and distracted we completely forgot our guide's caution to "check in." Fortunately, he saw that we had drifted too far from the safe zone and blew his whistle to get our attention. If he hadn't, we could have easily drifted farther and farther away until we "checked out."

It only takes a few seconds to lose focus, and when we lose focus, we drift into places we never dreamed we could go. Once there, we feel trapped, helpless, and hopeless. When couples fall in love and start a family, the dream is to live "happily ever after." We want to experience all the good things life has to offer. We want to be happy and thrive in our most important relationships. Unfortunately, even with the best of intentions, the demands of life and its unexpected twists and turns can cause us to drift away from the most important people in our lives. Busyness, stress, and pressures can negatively affect marriages and family relationships.

Maybe you're experiencing this in your marriage or with one of your children right now. Instead of being pulled closer together, you feel like you're moving further apart. You're in survival mode. You're coexisting, but there's little intimacy, connection, fulfillment, or joy in your home. You may not even know how it happened, but you're sure things aren't where they should be. You're in danger of *drift*.

THE DANGER SIGNS OF DRIFT

Drift can happen quickly when a relationship experiences a sudden shock, but far more often, it happens slowly, incrementally—so gradually that we don't even notice how far we've moved apart. The tension point for most of us—the time when we're most likely to drift—is when we've confused what we *naturally* want for what we *ultimately* want. We're programmed by the constant messages of our culture to long for *more*—to put our hopes in having *more*, doing *more*, and enjoying *more*. After all, we deserve it, right? In today's world, we can't quite be content with enough comfort, pleasure, success, or influence. More is what we *naturally* want. These things promise to fill our lives with a sense of accomplishment, peace, and happiness—and they do for a short time. But eventually they leave us empty, desperate, and confused. When this happens, drift is inevitable.

In contrast, our *ultimate* desires are for two essential things: significance and authentic relationships. If we have them, nothing can shake us. But if we don't, nothing will make us happy.

How can we tell if we're drifting? All we have to do is look at the people around us . . . and look in the mirror. Those who are drifting experience the following symptoms:

Disappointment: The heartaches of life crowd out the joys.

Regret: Past failures haunt us.

Isolation: Either others have pushed us away or we've chosen to distance ourselves from others so we'll feel safe.

Frustration: Everything is a grind, even the activities that used to bring joy.

Tension: We're always on edge, worried about what might come next.

These factors are evidence that we've lost focus and, as a result, our sense of significance and our confidence in others' genuine love and acceptance have been shaken. The good news is we don't have to live this way! Drift doesn't have to define us, and it doesn't have to ruin everything good in our lives—not anymore, at least. We can change. We can make strategic shifts.

FIVE SHIFTS

No matter what season of life you're in, we want to offer you a proven framework that will help you stop drifting and start living with greater intention. This framework is all about shifting back toward the people who matter most in your life—your family.

For nearly thirty years, we (Rodney and Michelle) have devoted our lives to helping people live with greater intention. One of the reasons we're so passionate about this topic is because we're as guilty as anyone of losing focus in our marriage and getting distracted by the responsibilities of work and raising children.

It's easy to preach to others on what they should do and not live the advice out yourself. We don't pretend to position ourselves or our family as "perfect" by any means. Trust us, we have made our share of mistakes like everyone else. We're fellow strugglers. If there's one thing that has helped us—and, honestly, saved us—in our marriage and family relationships, it's that we have a strong family legacy of faith. Without question, our faith has gotten us through many storms and has served as an anchor to our family.

We don't know what compelled you to pick up this book. Perhaps the title grabbed your attention, and you wondered what the whole "shift" thing was all about. Then again, maybe you are a husband, a wife, or a parent who is facing a real crisis in your home regarding your marriage or one of your kids. You might be desperate to figure out a way to save your family and get things moving in the right direction before it's too late. Maybe a friend or loved one gave you a copy of this book because it was helpful and encouraging, and that person wanted you to also benefit from the tools and 5-Step framework we're going to share. Regardless of the reason you're on this journey, we are going to walk through it together. Soon, yours will be among the hundreds of families—including our own—that have benefited from making the shift.

THE SHIFT BEGINS WITH YOU

In the five sections of this book, we'll look at five shifts we all need to make in *direction*, *focus*, *motivation*, *reinforcement*, and *purpose*. For each one, we'll provide hope and give you clear principles and practices to shift your family from where it is to where you want it to go.

The question is how? The only way to compensate for the drift and get moving again in the right direction is to make a shift by following these five steps:

Start with the end in mind.
Hold to core values.
Identify your GPS (Goals, Passions, and Struggles).
Find life-giving friendships.
Teach by example.

Whether your family is doing well and you want it to be even better, you're struggling and you need some practical help to get your family back on track, or you're at the end of your rope hanging on with everything you've got, you can make changes by taking them one step at a time. We're here to help you do just that and ultimately transform your most important relationships.

Are you ready? Let's stop the drift and make the shift.

Before you go any further, make this declaration of your firm intentions:

I declare a shift is coming—
A shift in my marriage.
A shift in my family relationships.
A shift in my priorities.
A shift in my future.

STEP 1

START WITH THE END IN MIND

A SHIFT IN DIRECTION

CHAPTER 1

ON YOUR MARK

Take an Honest Look
at Your Past and Present

You cannot change your destination overnight,
but you can change your direction overnight.
—Jim Rohn

One of the perks of living in Orlando is the convenience of being
able to drive over to the local attractions and theme parks for a
day of fun. One day, when our three kids, Becca, Ashlyn, and Luke,
were much younger, we decided to go to Disney's Magic Kingdom.
For some reason, we chose a day when half the population of the
planet was there.

Though we had to fight through the crowds for hours, our family
enjoyed a number of rides, shows, shops, and other amusements.
But when it was time for the next adventure, we gathered our clan
. . . and didn't see Luke. I (Rodney) scanned the immediate area.

Nothing. "You have Luke, don't you?" I asked Michelle. She shook her head, and when our eyes met, she instantly realized I didn't know where he was. I asked the girls, "Have you seen Luke?" Nope. Now all of us were in full-blown panic mode!

We searched the area like crazy people but couldn't find him anywhere. News reports of missing and kidnapped children flashed in our minds—well, Michelle's and mine, not the girls'. After a long and frantic but empty search, we asked one of the cast members at Disney World where a missing child might be taken. He pointed us to something like a human lost and found department. To our relief, when we got there, we found Luke, who looked as though nothing in the world was wrong. It was a joy-filled reunion. I didn't let him get more than a foot away from me the rest of the day.

FAMILY DRIFT

It's easy to lose something you value, like a child, a marriage, a family relationship, or even a dream you've held in your heart for years. Wise parents acknowledge that even in the best of families, things can go wrong—sometimes much quicker than could ever be expected.

Research shows most people still believe the family is an important and essential institution. Barna Group states: "Family is ranked by American adults as more central to their identity than any other surveyed factor (i.e. being an American, faith, ethnicity, etc.). More than six in 10 (62%) also say that family plays a significant role in their identity."[1] But the numbers also show a steady decline in each generation. While 76 percent of those belonging to the silent generation (1928–1945) said that family made up "a lot" of their identity, among the boomers (1946–1964), that number dropped to 64 percent; for Gen-Xers (1965–1980) it was 61 percent, and the millennials (1981–1996) came in at only 53 percent.[2] It doesn't take a math whiz to detect a disturbing trend here.

As family coaches, we can't think of a better term than *drift* to describe the growing threat we see among families in our culture today. It describes exactly what happens to most married couples, and it always affects their kids. Couples usually start with firm commitments to strong, loving relationships based on spiritual and moral foundations. But at some point, without even realizing it, parents begin to focus more and more on their work schedules and financial demands, their kids become more involved in academic requirements and extracurricular activities, and the once close-knit family finds itself at various stages of emotional distance. Some need only a little shift to get back on track, but others need an extreme home makeover!

We believe most families start out with the best of intentions, but the snorkeling "check in" rule applies here too. The excitement of having children and enjoying all the developmental stages of their young lives, coupled with the many time-consuming responsibilities of parenthood, can cause parents to move into survival mode. Over time, imperceptibly, the increasing demands of work, financial pressure, and endless busyness create a dangerous drift away from the family connections that once seemed unbreakable. When family members fail to regularly raise their heads to "check in" and see where they are spiritually, morally, and relationally, they eventually drift further away from God and His plans and purposes for their family. They "check out" and begin to drown in the sea of problems: family conflict, wayward kids, marriage trouble, and, quite often, divorce.

This is the point when we (Rodney and Michelle) get a phone call. A marriage or a child is drowning and the family is crying out for help. They've found themselves drifting away from the security and satisfaction they once shared in the home. Now they wonder if rescue is even possible. Sadly, this condition has become the norm, not the exception.

> Your current situation is not your family's final destination.
> —RODNEY AND MICHELLE GAGE

In all our years of working with students and families, here's what we know to be true: *Your direction, not your intention, will lead you to your destination.* In other words, no matter how sincerely you intend to raise spiritually and morally strong kids, it doesn't just happen. The truth is, the direction your marriage and family are moving right now along the path you have set with your values, commitments, and priorities will ultimately determine your destination.

In our roles, we see many young parents highly involved in their children's lives when they start school. The parents volunteer, show up for parent-teacher meetings, and donate money for worthy causes to help the school and community. In addition, they sign their children up for all kinds of extracurricular activities: Little League, Boy Scouts and Girl Scouts, dance, cheerleading, music lessons . . . the list goes on and on. Clearly, the parents' intentions are heartfelt. They want the very best for their children.

As the kids grow up, their activities demand even more time and money. In addition, academic priorities become a consuming focus. Parents discover that most of the better public and private universities look for a high-achieving record of accomplishments before a child will even be considered for acceptance. Consequently, parents experience a tremendous amount of tension trying to balance the demands of school, all the extracurricular activities, work schedules, and basic household responsibilities.

You already know this, of course—or, if your kids are still very young, you'll find out soon enough. The point is that we need more than good intentions for raising strong families. Intentions won't prevent drift. We need to assess and address the direction we're moving. Are we allowing drift to gradually take us away from where we really want to be? Or are we making a persistent effort to stop the drift, recalculate, and do whatever it takes to move back in a direction that will take us to a place where we and our kids thrive?

LOOK UP AND LOOK AROUND

An old saying tells us, "If you keep doing the same thing you've always done, you'll keep getting the same results you've always gotten." Once you realize that drift has become a problem in your family, and especially if you detect that you are continuing to drift with no control over the situation, it's time for you to act—to do something different.

There are people for whom drift is inevitable. They may have grown up in broken homes, with absent parents or single parents, in unloving foster care homes, or without any understanding of what having a loving, strong family could look like. But from our interactions with thousands of people, we've identified six primary reasons families drift—no matter the familial background or good intentions. These can be present to a minor or major degree, and adults may experience one or more of them at the same time:

1. They don't have a clear vision of what family life can be.

    All they've seen when it comes to relationships—whether their parents' relationship, their family's relationships with extended family, or the relationships among other families—is people who barely tolerate one another, people whose anger leads to explosions or implosions, and people with a goal only to survive another day without too much trauma or drama.

2. They don't have a set of guiding values that shape their decisions and interactions.

They've absorbed their values—that is, what's most important to them—from their parents and from the culture, and they've never even considered outlining how they can relate to one another.

3. They confuse their commitments with their priorities.

They've made commitments of time and energy to various activities before establishing a list of things to be prioritized and eliminating other things.

4. They don't do enough to protect their family from powerful, though often attractive, negative influences.

They've viewed the culture's supreme values of success, pleasure, and approval as perfectly reasonable because they're so pervasive.

5. They focus on one another's faults instead of strengths.

They're hurt people who hurt people. Empty and wounded, they've become as prickly as porcupines!

6. Their deepest needs for security and love aren't met, so they operate out of a deficiency instead of an overflow of gratitude.

They've failed to look deeper—to uncover the truths about their wounds and highest desires and experience God's love, forgiveness, and strength.

Do any of these sound familiar?

Let's return to the lesson we learned while snorkeling: If you were swimming in the ocean and realized that drift had become a serious threat, you'd take action and change direction. Ironically, most of us are probably better prepared to handle a crisis at sea than the problem of drift in our own homes. Ocean swimmers have a plan; they're taught that in the event a riptide starts to carry them out to sea, they shouldn't panic. They shouldn't attempt a mad swim directly back to shore against the strong current. Instead, they're instructed to swim parallel to the shore until they get out of the potentially deadly current, and then swim diagonally toward the shore to safety. Likewise we must have a plan for our families.

THINK *WHO* BEFORE *DO*

We believe there are two crucial questions all of us need to ask ourselves:

1. Who do I want to be as a husband or wife and as a parent?

    Far too often, husbands and wives lose their sense of vision, purpose, and meaning, so the best they can imagine is to struggle through another day with as little hassle as possible. The currents of the culture sweep them downstream. They're drifting, but they don't even notice. They become wrapped up in secondary things and miss the most important things. When we treasure those things above God and His purposes, we become vulnerable to temptation and deception. And with technology, our kids are exposed to far more negative influences than we could have ever imagined when we were in school. Soon, the feeling of regret replaces their passion for life.

    It may help to expand this question into specifics. Together, you should answer: Who do we want to be as a couple? Who do we want to be as a family? And individually: Who do I want to be as a mom or dad? You start to regain a vision by asking these questions . . . and spending plenty of time answering them. Once we understand who we want to be, we can then focus on what we need to do.

2. Is there a desire gap between how things are now and what I feel "ought" to be?

After you've answered the first question, this one focuses on the challenge of change. Your gap may be large or small, but whatever the size, we all need tangible steps and fuel for our passions to motivate us to close the desire gap in our lives. The deepest issues in our lives aren't the words we use when we talk to each other, but the source of those words. Jesus said, "Out of the abundance of the heart [the] mouth speaks" (Luke 6:45 NKJV). Change is the bridge between who you are and who you want to become. Based upon whom you desire to be, you will need to make changes and stop certain behaviors. Shifting takes courage.

When we get our *who* right, we get our *what* right!
—RODNEY AND MICHELLE GAGE

We'll be honest with you: The sooner you notice the effects of drift on your family, the easier it is to make the adjustments and get back on course. But we suspect that many people have picked up this book because they're in various stages of going under. The longer we wait to acknowledge drift, the more it can pull us down spiritually, morally, emotionally, relationally, and financially. If that's your case, let us assure you: It's never too late to make a shift that will restore your family to peaceful waters and smooth sailing.

IT'S NEVER TOO LATE

We've had the privilege of seeing God work in the lives of individuals, couples, and families to bring dramatic and lasting change. Here are just a few examples:

- Suzanne is a single mother who felt traumatized by her husband's infidelity and unwillingness to make any changes in his priorities. A year after they divorced, she could barely make it through work each day, and she had very little energy left for her two children, eight and twelve years old. She joined a group that helped her experience God's love, grieve her deep hurts, and find God's purpose for her as a daughter of the King and as a mother. Today, she is one of the most joyful people we know.

- Jarod and Alicia scheduled two appointments, one with a counselor and the other with an attorney. If the first appointment didn't go well, they were going to go to the attorney to get a divorce. Both Jarod and Alicia had good jobs, but they had spent far beyond their income. The strain of trying to pay interest on their debt each month caused them to blame each other, and their kids were often the objects of their anger. The counselor gave them hope that their matrix of problems—debt, marital stress, and children out of control—could be resolved in a process of healing, a commitment to speak to one another with grace, and finding a financial counselor. Hope had a miraculous effect. They soon were talking to each other with respect, they didn't bark at their children, and they began to see light at the end of the financial tunnel.

- Jenny had been physically and emotionally abused by her father, so she had great difficulty trusting men, including her husband, Robert. She was emotionally fragile; anything less than complete and perfect affection offended her and caused her to withdraw. Poor Robert never saw this coming. Before they married, he knew Jenny had some problems with her father, but when she finally told him the truth, her

17

behavior made a lot more sense. Together, they found a way forward, discovering deeper love and security than either of them had ever known before.

- Carlos and Maria had enjoyed the good life before they had kids. They traveled, Carlos fished, and Maria liked her work and had frequent lunches with friends. They assumed having kids would fit nicely into their priorities, but it didn't. The demands of parenthood challenged Carlos and Maria and made them irritable with each other and with their little children. When they finally realized their resentment was ruining their family, they decided to get help. They met with an older couple who had weathered many storms in their marriage, and the more mature couple helped Carlos and Maria reframe their expectations. Finally, Carlos and Maria had something bigger and better to live for than fun.

We could describe countless other couples and families struggling with everything from the normal strains of life to the ravages of addiction, depression, debt, abuse, and isolation. We talk to men and women who have tried to find solace in the arms of someone other than a spouse. The pursuit was thrilling for a while, but it devastated their marriages and their kids. We know families who smile and look put together on the outside but behind closed doors suffer from outbursts of rage and shattered hearts. Pornography is so common that it has become an epidemic, even in the Christian community. Some say that it's harmless; we know it's anything but. It reshapes the viewer's perspective of sexuality and causes them to be dissatisfied with anything but attractive and seductive people—unlike anyone they're with. We've seen parents push their kids to excel in academics and sports so they can get into the best schools and win scholarships. If those kids do get in, they enter a world of even more pressure, and if they don't, they're crushed by a failure they assume will ruin their lives.

If there's one thing we (Rodney and Michelle) are known for, beyond the love we have for each other and our three children, it's our passion to see families challenge the norm by living with greater intention. Through the years, I (Rodney) have had the opportunity to speak to millions of teenagers through school assemblies. Michelle and I have worked with hundreds of couples and families whose lives and relationships have tragically fallen apart. Why are we telling you this? Because our experience is evidence that raising spiritually, emotionally, morally strong and secure children and having a healthy, thriving marriage doesn't just happen. As a matter of fact, I believe it's more difficult for marriages and families to thrive in today's culture—spiritually, morally, and relationally—than ever before.

That's why we're convinced families suffering from drift need more than just prayer; they need a plan. Knowing what to do can help you close the distance between where you are now and where you want to be as a family. The 5-Step Plan we're using as a framework for this book is based on the trials and errors, as well as successes, we ourselves have experienced. Other parents have helped us along the way by sharing their wisdom and advice, which we'll pass along too. Our family, families in our church, and families across the country have field tested this plan and proven that we don't have to keep perpetuating the same hurts, habits, and hang-ups. We don't have to pass them on to our children. With God's help, we can make the shift. No matter what you've encountered in the past, or what your current situation is, this book will give you the opportunity to recapture your hopes and dreams.

Yesterday ended last night. Tomorrow's pages are blank. Today, you can begin to make an improvement in your marriage and family. We're praying for you that God will bring healing to your past and reconciliation and restoration to your relationships today. We believe God can use you and your family in ways you never thought possible. We have no doubt that He can turn your pain into a platform to tell a new story about you and your family.

That's why we're convinced families suffering from drift need more than just prayer; they need a plan.

—RODNEY AND MICHELLE GAGE

THE LAW OF DIMINISHING INTENT

The late Jim Rohn was a business consultant, author, and speaker who offered valuable insights that translate into every area of life. One of his most important discoveries, the "law of diminishing intent," states: "The longer you wait to do something you should do now, the greater the odds that you will never actually do it."[3] You instinctively know it's true: When you know the right thing to do, the longer you wait, the more excuses, new roadblocks, and apathy seem to appear. Initial enthusiasm and conviction can soon lapse into "It was a good idea" and then become "Why was I even thinking about that?"

Every chapter in this book has action points—specific things you and your family can do to identify your purpose and pursue it with all your heart. But know this: You'll want to wait, you'll come up with reasons it won't matter, and you'll assume your spouse or kids will be so resistant that every attempt is just a waste of time. Don't believe it! *Lean into action.* Sure, you'll make some mistakes, but you'll learn from them. If you sit on the bench, you'll never score any points. It's safer to sit out, but it leads to a life of discontent and emptiness. I hope you'll realize you can take steps forward as you read every page. Take them. Don't wait, or your intent and your enthusiasm will gradually waste away. And then the only thing that will change is an increase in discouragement.

Some of us are afraid of our desires because they've been shattered so often before, but don't be afraid of your desire for a loving, healthy family. This longing is the first step in leaving a legacy for generations to come. Our prayer is that this book will prompt you to experience a shift unlike anything you have ever known. As you continue reading, keep in mind God's challenge and God's promise from Isaiah, a prophet who lived over 2,500 years ago:

> "Forget about what's happened; don't keep going over old history. Be alert, be present. I'm about to do something brand-new. It's bursting out! Don't you see it? There it is! I'm making a road through the desert, rivers in the badlands." (Isaiah 43:18–19 MSG)

As Jesus began His ministry, He also read from the book of Isaiah and proclaimed: "This is God's year to act!" (Luke 4:16–21 MSG). Not next year. Not five or ten years from now. We believe *this* is the year God will help you shift your most important relationships in a new direction.

By the way, we're not assuming you know your way around the Bible. We believe it is the source of wisdom and encouragement that God uses to transform individuals and families. We're using a number of different translations to make the points as clear as possible. We have built our lives, values, and beliefs on the book Jesus fulfilled and validated as God's Word to us, and we're sure God will use it in your life too. Let's be clear: Most of what you'll read in this book is countercultural. It's different from the assumptions the vast majority of people make each day. God's Word is encouraging because it tells us about God's amazing grace, forgiveness, and love, but it also challenges us to see things from God's point of view and take action based on His values.

God created the family. It's His idea. In the Bible, He has given us a blueprint to follow as we build strong families that can resist the constant push of the culture's current. So, as you read passages from the Bible in these pages, open your heart to hear from God Himself. He's speaking to you through His Word.

At the end of each chapter, you'll find some questions designed to stimulate personal reflection and interaction with your spouse and perhaps a small group of couples who recognize the need to make a shift. The goal isn't to get through them as quickly as possible but to let them spark analysis (in the "Think About It" sections) and a commitment to take bold steps forward (when you're prompted to "Do It").

 THINK ABOUT IT:

1. If you could only use five words to describe your childhood family, what would they be?
2. Did growing up in your family create any unhealthy habits or behaviors that you have since overcome? Are you aware of any lingering habits that still need to be addressed and corrected?
3. What are some examples of drift you've witnessed in today's culture (in politics, education, churches, etc.)?
4. What are the forces and temptations that cause drift in families? Which of these have been a problem for your family?

5. How frequently do you "check in" to see if you have drifted from God's plan and purpose for your life? When was the last time you checked in for an honest analysis?

6. If you're reading this book, you have good intentions. Would you also say you have a destination in mind? If so, what is it? (And if not, the next chapter will help you think it through.)

 DO IT:

Answer and discuss these questions with your spouse:

1. Who do I want to be as a husband or wife and as a parent?

2. What does the "desire gap" look like for me and my family?

CHAPTER 2

GET SET

Create a Family Mission and Vision

It's just as difficult to reach a destination you don't have,
as it is to come back from a place you've never been.

—ZIG ZIGLAR

In our book *ReThink Life*, I (Rodney) share an embarrassing moment that took place several years ago at my son's class field trip to Jungle Adventures, one of Florida's original theme parks. At the time, Luke was bound to a wheelchair, so his teacher permitted us to drive separately. She told us to follow the yellow school buses to the park. I was sure the day would create a lot of fun memories for Luke and me.

I didn't bother to get directions because there was no way to lose a big yellow bus, but Luke's teacher gave me her cell phone number just in case we got separated. As we approached a major intersection, I decided to go around the bus in front of us so Luke could wave to his friends. When I pulled back into the lane, we were in front of the bus we'd been following, but still behind several others lined up at a stoplight. The light turned green, and the buses in front of us turned right and drove up the interstate on-ramp. I followed them, even though it seemed a bit odd that the buses behind us went straight instead of turning right. I didn't give it much thought; I was confident I was doing the right thing by following the buses in front of me.

But soon, doubts began to surface. What if we were supposed to have gone with the other buses? This *was* the way to Jungle Adventures, wasn't it? Unwavering in my resolve to keep trailing the yellow buses, about thirty minutes later I followed the group into a parking lot with a huge alligator head beside a sign that read "Gatorland." With a perplexed look on his face, Luke exclaimed, "Wait a minute, Dad! This is not where our class is going! We're supposed to be at Jungle Adventures."

About that time, my cell phone rang. Luke's teacher asked, "Did you get lost?"

I stammered, "We're, uh, at Gatorland!" Luke and I raced across town to join his class. I'd done exactly what I thought was right, but it was very wrong. I'd followed the buses, but I'd followed the *wrong* buses.

Without a specific destination in mind—as an individual or as part of a family, business, nonprofit, church, etc.—you're always at risk of drift. So now, let me ask: Do you know where you want to go as a family? Is your family going somewhere *on purpose*? Do you have a specific destination—distinct goals—in mind for your family relationships? Or are you perhaps following the wrong bus?

The key to experiencing a relationally and spiritually strong family is to start with the end in mind. Starting does require asking some tough, reflective questions. Where do you see your marriage in the future? What kind of marriage do you want to have? How will you stay devoted and faithful to each other through challenging seasons such as raising children and growing professionally? What do you want for your children's futures? What kind of people do you want them to become as they enter their teens and adulthood? How will they learn to avoid temptations? How will they learn to make wise choices? The potential dangers of not answering these questions are why it's so important to start with the end in mind. We've already made the point, but we want to emphasize it again: Every family *ends up somewhere*, but few *end up somewhere on purpose*.

THE IMPORTANCE OF MISSION AND VISION

We usually think of the words *mission* and *vision* in a business context, but every good endeavor needs crystal clear direction. Scripture gives us fair warning: "Where there is no vision, the people perish" (Proverbs 29:18 KJV). A more recent interpretation puts it this way: "If people can't see what God is doing, they stumble all over themselves" (MSG). In other words, when people lose their "why," they lose their way.

It has always amazed us how major companies and nonprofits invest time and money in writing both a mission statement (to explain why the organization exists) and a vision statement (to define where they want to go), yet when it comes to the most important institution God created—the family—we seem to just cross our fingers and hope for the best. No wonder so many married couples, kids, and families "stumble all over themselves."

Ask yourself if what you are doing today is getting you closer to where you want to be tomorrow.
—DR. DAVE MARTIN

Having a clearly stated mission and vision for your life, marriage, and family will provide four key benefits:

1. Passion: Our purpose is fueled by our passion. When we have a clear mission and vision for our marriages and families, we feel energized and empowered to make them happen. The opposite of love isn't hate; it's apathy. When we lose our passion for God and the people He has given us to love and protect, we become complacent. We begin to take each other for granted, and we find ourselves merely coexisting, which leads to drifting. Knowing your "why" and keeping it in front of you will fuel your passion to live intentionally every day.

2. Motivation: Life is hard. Having a healthy and thriving marriage and a close-knit family is difficult to achieve in today's culture. However, when we have a clear mission and vision for what *should* be and *could* be for our families, we're motivated to keep fighting for what matters most. It's easy to feel overwhelmed and discouraged. A clear mission and vision will give us the motivation we need to push through the difficulties in life.

3. Direction: When you start with the end in mind, you always have a north star to guide you. It will keep you from following the wrong bus. Of course, we all get off track at times. We may even get completely turned around. But a clear vision statement works like a compass to help us continually adjust our course and start moving again in the right direction.

4. Purpose: Life is too short to live only for ourselves and things that are secondary (at best). We were made for more. We were made to make a difference. If your family has a pulse, it has a purpose. Your family was not meant to merely survive; it was meant to thrive! Jesus said, "The thief comes only to steal and kill and destroy; I have come that they may have life, and have it to the full" (John 10:10).

ANYONE AND EVERYONE

It's never too early to get serious about putting together a family mission and vision statement . . . and it's never too late! Couples with young children are certainly at a prime time to initiate a discussion of why the family exists and what future goals they want to work toward. As the children grow, they will always have those guidelines to keep them grounded and growing. However, *anyone* can benefit from creating a mission and vision statement:

- *Singles* can get an early start on considering future goals. Identifying their desired destination is the best way to find like-minded and spiritually compatible people to share their lives with. And if they remain single, they need a clear and compelling sense of purpose to make life exciting and fulfilling.
- *Couples without kids* can benefit from having a plan in place before kids enter the picture and "extra" time suddenly disappears. Quite often, a pregnancy prompts couples to dream about what their family can become. Those months are a great time to think about, plan for, imagine, and pray about the future.
- *Even empty nesters* and *grandparents* should consider, "What kind of legacy do I want to leave my family?" These people have time on their hands again, so they can fill it by being a positive influence for those they care most about.

My (Michelle's) dad has four daughters and eleven grandkids, and he stays busy going from one place to another. Every time we get together, he gathers us all, sits us down, and lets us know he prays for us every day by name, specifically for three things: God's *presence*, God's *protection*, and God's *provision* for our lives. Then he asks the kids to repeat back what he has just said. We always leave with this reminder and a better understanding of why we exist as a family. Our spiritual growth is his legacy. To quote Andy Stanley: "Your greatest contribution to the kingdom of God may not be something you do but someone you raise."[1]

The psalmist tells us: "Take delight in the LORD, and he will give you your heart's desires. Commit everything you do to the LORD. Trust him, and he will help you" (Psalm 37:4–5 NLT). God does not attach age limitations. It's never too soon to start considering your heart's desires. It's never too late to revisit what is most important to you. If you've crafted a mission statement and a vision statement for an organization, transfer the process to write one for your family. And if you've never created these statements, let us help you get started.

Your family was not meant to merely survive;
it was meant to thrive!
—RODNEY AND MICHELLE GAGE

WRITING YOUR MISSION AND VISION STATEMENTS

Your mission statement and vision statement should work hand in hand. Each addresses a specific question, and they complement one another.

As you can see from the diagram on the following page, there are actually four components to this planning process: mission, values, vision, and strategy. We've found it helpful at first to narrow the focus to two: mission and vision. Values shape our mission, and strategy fleshes out the vision, but we'll focus primarily on the main two, because if we get those right, the others will follow fairly easily.

Your family mission statement should answer the question, "Why do I (or we) exist?" As you live and grow together, you need to determine your goals for your life and future. Another way to ask this is, "What impact will we have on each other now, and what legacy will we leave for our children, grandchildren, and future generations?" You'll probably come up with more than one answer or have multiple sentences. That's great, but make sure it's not too cumbersome and complicated. The mission statement needs to fit easily on the back of a business card. If it's too long or too complex, keep working on it until it's easy to remember. If it's not memorable, it's not going to be captured in your heart.

Since this statement is a family document, each member should weigh in about what's important to them. Younger children will have more simplistic goals, and teenagers are more ambitious, but you need all of those responses to create a mission statement that applies to everyone in the family.

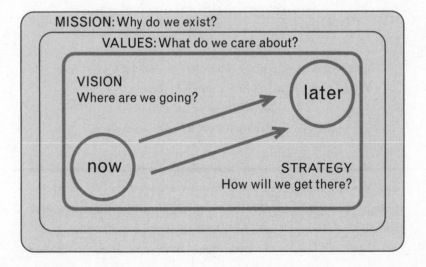

In planning anything, the best place to begin is at the end.
What outcome do you want?
—MICHAEL HYATT AND DANIEL HARKAVY

The process is as important—and maybe *more* important—than the outcome. Don't be in too much of a hurry to get something down on paper. It's possible to sit down and write out a mission statement in a few minutes, but it's much better to have a series of family discussions and let your mission naturally evolve from your questions and interactions. If you don't put a lot of thought into writing it, family members probably won't value it as a guide.

To give you an example, here is our family's mission statement, but feel free to create your own format or design:

THE GAGE FAMILY MISSION STATEMENT
The Gage family exists to *Love, Lead, Learn, Laugh,* and *Live:*
Love God and others the way God loves us;
Lead by example in order to use our influence to make
a difference in people's lives;
Learn from our successes and mistakes: Failure is never final;
Laugh and have fun. Don't take ourselves so seriously.
Make others smile; and
Live each day to its fullest; live with no regrets.

After your *mission* statement defines "Why do we exist?" the family *vision* statement should answer the question, "Where are we going?" The mission statement is the big idea; the vision statement should be a more practical, hands-on application of the mission.

Again, all family members should have input into the creation of the vision statement. Their contribution helps them understand the power of the vision to give motivation and direction. The more personal this statement is, the more practical it will be. Here is our family's vision statement:

THE GAGE FAMILY VISION STATEMENT

Our vision is to be a family that lives differently from the norm by standing up and standing out for Jesus so that we will win others to Christ and continue our family's legacy for generations to come.

A clear vision can provide confidence to stand firm on your beliefs, values, and decisions, especially when they're different from the norm of our mainstream culture. Your vision will almost certainly attract critics and naysayers. We call those people *vision vandals*. But your clear vision fueled with a passion for what should be will give you the determination to see that vision become a reality.

When our daughter Becca became a freshman in high school, she tried out for the cheerleading team, and she made it. I (Michelle) was really proud of her, but I found out fast that the other moms took cheerleading a lot more seriously than we did. They insisted on having control of every aspect of the girls' lives, and of course, they didn't always agree with each other. I guess that is why some people referred to the moms as "drama mamas."

Being on the team is very competitive, and for the girls who make it, it can be very exclusive. About the time Becca was beginning her cheerleading practices, she also found a passion to help lead singing in our church's youth group. The conflict of time was an issue, but so was the conflict of values. After a while, one passion grew and the other ebbed away. Becca decided to drop off the cheerleading team after her freshman year and focus her time and energy on music.

Immediately, some of the other girls treated her like she had leprosy. Following her heart caused Becca to pay a price in her relationships, but she wasn't the only one. Some of the parents of girls on the team treated us with the same contempt. They felt betrayed because our daughter had a mind of her own and chose to do something else with her life. This situation told us a lot about Becca's character. A compelling vision is a yes to one thing and a no to anything that competes with it.

A vision without a strategy is just wishing, so the final part of the process is crafting a strategy to fulfill the family vision. A family strategy answers the question, "How do we get there?" This aspect is even more specific, with clear goals, a timeline, and an understanding of the resources needed to reach the goals.

The only thing worse than being blind
is having sight but no vision.
—HELEN KELLER

THE POWER OF VISION

Monty Roberts tells a story that demonstrates the power of vision. He became a world-renowned expert on horse training, but not without some serious challenges along the way. During Monty's senior year in high school, one of his teachers, Mr. Fowler, gave an assignment. He instructed his students to write a paper titled "My Goals in Life," detailing what they envisioned for themselves. He told them, "It should be like painting a picture of your lives in the future, as if all your ambitions had been realized." But Mr. Fowler added a caveat: "This vision should be realistic. I don't want to hear about some crazy, off-the-wall plan."

Monty's father was a horse trainer, and Monty had been around horses all his young life. Since age nine he had been drawing stables and training facilities. He confidently turned in a paper to Mr. Fowler with a detailed plan to build a thoroughbred racehorse facility. Monty was stunned five days later when his teacher returned the paper with a big red F at the top. When Monty went to talk to him about the grade, his teacher justified it because he felt Monty had ignored the instruction to be realistic. Mr. Fowler knew Monty didn't come from a wealthy family and said, "It's a wild, unattainable dream." But he gave Monty the opportunity to revise the paper and turn it in again to avoid a failing grade.

After seeing Monty struggle several days with this assignment, his mother offered her support. She told him if he thought it was an unattainable dream, he should change his paper. But if he really believed he could accomplish his goal, he should just resubmit the paper with no changes and live with the consequences. That's what he did. He turned his paper back in along with a note telling Mr. Fowler that he could grade the paper as he wished, but he had no right to limit his aspirations. Monty never found out what grade he made on that paper, but his final grades in the mail at the end of the year revealed he had made an A in the class.[2]

Monty went on to achieve his goals and established Flag Is Up Farms, a sprawling ranch (very much like the one he had described in high school) in Solvang, California, devoted to the care and training of thoroughbred horses. Many years after his high school graduation, he received an unexpected call from Mr. Fowler, who had retired and was the social director of his church group. He wanted to know if he could bring a group of seniors to tour Monty's ranch, so Monty arranged a time.

When the bus arrived, Mr. Fowler was the first one off, and he greeted Monty warmly. Many of the older group members weren't very mobile and needed to view the facility from the bus, but Monty had ensured that plenty of horses were training nearby for them to see. After the tour, Mr. Fowler publicly acknowledged that although he had been Monty's teacher, Monty had taught him an important lesson: "A teacher does not have the right to put a cap on the aspirations of his students, no matter how unreal those aspirations might seem."[3]

Monty's vision had been strong enough to endure inaccurate criticism, even from an early age. It was what gave him direction and passion. When your family establishes a vision and commits to it, the vision will become an anchor that provides stability to withstand the pressures, heartaches, and criticisms we all suffer from time to time.

NOT ONLY DIRECTION
BUT REDIRECTION

Because mission and vision provide ongoing direction, they are invaluable during those times when we temporarily lose our focus or stray from our intended path—in other words, when we drift. They don't just start us down the right road; they help us find our way back when we get turned around. All families—ours included—get off track from time to time, sometimes quite literally.

A few years ago, all my (Michelle's) extended family vacationed together in Steamboat Springs, Colorado. It was a collection of nieces, nephews, kids, and grandkids—a whole army of people. We stayed in a beautiful location, and one day everybody loaded up in the cars and drove to a spot where we started a long climb up a mountain. By the time we got to the top and had taken in the magnificent scenery, we were tired. Almost everyone decided to take the gondola back down, but Rodney and I had heard there was a walking trail down to the base of the mountain that was only about a three-mile hike. We figured that wouldn't be a problem, so we, along with our daughter Ashlyn, decided to walk back. We waved to the rest of the family as they descended in the gondola, and we started down the trail.

Along the trek, we noticed our path led us away from the overhead gondola. We assumed it wasn't a big deal. We were sure we'd come out next to the bottom terminal of the gondola. Wrong. When we arrived at the base of the mountain, we discovered we were five miles away from where we had intended to be! Several hours later and completely exhausted, we finally caught up with the rest of the family. The next day, our muscle cramps and sore ankles reminded Rodney, Ashlyn, and me of our long detour. I learned an important lesson through that experience: Even though we had gotten way off course, the reason we were able to get back on track was that we knew our ultimate destination.

A lot of people like to quote Jeremiah 29:11: "'For I know the plans I have for you,' declares the LORD, 'plans to prosper you and not to harm you, plans to give you hope and a future.'" It's a wonderful promise. Who wouldn't want this kind of assurance from God? But many people don't realize that this promise came at perhaps the lowest point in Israel's long history—and they'd had several low points. Jeremiah was passing along God's message that, because of the people's stubbornness and continued participation in idolatry, God was removing His blessing from them. Jerusalem, their cherished capital city, had been destroyed by the Babylonians, who had also leveled their temple and taken many Israelites to Babylon as captives. There, they lived in exile in a state of emotional and spiritual despair (see Psalm 137).

In the middle of their heartache, Jeremiah relayed God's promise that Babylon wasn't their final destination. They were enduring a time of struggle and disappointment, but God was still in charge. They had wandered off track and were suffering for it, but their dismal times would come to an end. Someday, they would return to their homeland. Jeremiah was urging his people to start with the end in mind. It was a message that was hard for them to hear, but it would help them endure. And everything happened just as God had said.

The way we choose to get to where we're going defines what it's going to be like when we get there.
—SETH GODIN

FIRST STEP, NEXT STEP

The first step in getting to where you want to be as a family is knowing where you want to go as a family, which is why a mission statement and vision statement are essential. So for now, put your time and effort into analyzing, dreaming about, discussing, praying over, and creating your family mission and vision statements. Before you go any further in this process, you need to have the end in mind. Drift isn't inevitable—at least, not for long. If you invest in identifying your family's purpose and direction, you'll be on the right path, and when you realize you're drifting, you'll know how to get back on track. In Proverbs 14, the wise King Solomon warned us: "You can rationalize it all you want and justify the path of error you have chosen, but you'll find out in the end that you took the road to destruction" (v. 12 TPT).

In our role working with all kinds of families, we often try to imagine what it would be like if everyone in our homes, churches, and communities stopped resisting what God has shown is best for them and found meaning, joy, and fulfillment in following Him with all their hearts. What would the world look like if everyone quit being content with "survival mode" and instead committed to thriving in their relationships and growing spiritually? What if each of us started living the full life God created us to experience? We like to quote this insight to families who come to us looking to make a shift: "Small tweaks will take you to giant peaks."[4] If there was ever a time for families to make the shift, we believe it's now. Every family ends up somewhere. Is your family going wherever life takes you? Or are you going somewhere *on purpose*?

 THINK ABOUT IT:

1. Is your family most in need of passion, motivation, direction, or purpose? How do you plan to strengthen any weak areas?

2. At this stage in your life, what would be the value of creating (or reviewing) mission and vision statements for you or your family?

3. When is the best time for you to get started? (The sooner the better! Check the schedules of everyone who needs to be involved, and block off time on the calendar.)

4. Do you anticipate any resistance? If you do, how will you handle it?

5. Do you feel pressured to tightly control the process? If you do, how can you relax and invite people to participate in their own way?

6. How would you describe a family that's thriving? Can you give examples of families you know or examples of families in books you've read or in the Bible?

7. How would you describe a family that is merely surviving?

8. How would you rate your own family: as surviving, thriving, or somewhere in between? Explain your answer.

DO IT:

1. Have your initial family conversation to get input about your mission and vision.
2. After you talk, write your first versions down.

CHAPTER 3

GO!

Commit to Practical First Steps

Your commitments can develop you or destroy you,
but either way, they will define you.

—RICK WARREN

There are two kinds of people in this world—those who like jig-saw puzzles and those who don't. I (Rodney) fall into the camp of not liking jigsaw puzzles because they require too much time and patience. On the other hand, Michelle loves them. To her, sitting down and working on a puzzle is not only therapeutic but also a way to enjoy meaningful conversation. Working on a puzzle with some-one or as a family allows you to work toward a common goal.

Have you ever stopped to think about what the most impor-tant part of a puzzle is? It's not any certain puzzle piece, but with-out this one critical component, you almost certainly wouldn't be able to complete the puzzle. Curious as to what it is? It's the box top! Without having a clear picture of what you're attempting to put together, working on a puzzle can become one of the most frustrating experiences of your life. Even if you get lucky in finding a few pieces to fit together, over time, you'll probably end up throwing in the towel and quitting. The puzzle will be incomplete.

That is a picture of how most people live their lives—they try to put the pieces together without even knowing what their life, marriage, or family is supposed to look like.

In the previous chapters, we discussed the importance of having a clear mission and vision and how these keep us from drifting in our most important relationships. When we have a clear picture of what that is and why it is important it can change the trajectory of individuals, marriages, families, and generations to come. But having the "box top" doesn't necessarily mean that the puzzle is going to be a piece of cake. Putting hundreds or even thousands of puzzle pieces together still requires patience, focus, communication, and teamwork. Still, knowing your "box top" picture and what you're wanting to accomplish can make all the difference in the world. A clear picture of your mission and vision (your "why") will motivate what you do as you strive to fulfill God's plans and purposes for your life and family.

A goal is not about what you accomplish.
It's about what you become.
—MICHAEL HYATT

TAILORED MOTIVATION

Each member of our families may have very different fuels of motivation to keep them going. Some are inspired by encouragement and recognition, and others find inspiration in the immensity of the challenge. The thought of a far-future benefit gets some engines revving, and others prefer when they can envision immediate gain. Some desire the prospect of personal advancement, and for others, the opportunity to have an impact far beyond themselves is what matters most.

This point may surprise you: Some of the people joining you on this journey to stop the drift are probably not exactly like you, and they don't think exactly like you do! If you try to force square pegs in your round hole of motivation, all will be frustrated, and at least one of you will probably quit. And even one person not being involved in the family's purpose is a huge downer; all the empty spaces need to be put together to complete the picture.

The first task of any communicator is to know your audience. Yes, the person sleeping next to you and the ones who are in bed down the hall are your audience for your "vision talk." The question is, Do you know what captures the minds and hearts of each person? Can you tell when their eyes glaze over and when they sit up with anticipation? Have you learned what deflates each one and what makes each feel inspired and energized? If you can't answer those questions, it's not a hopeless situation. You just need to talk and listen more than ever to your family members during this process of crafting your mission and vision.

Remember, opposites attract . . . and too often, opposites attack! A wise person has the ability to enter other people's worlds—to understand what they value, how they think, how long they take to make decisions, and what makes their eyes light up. Presentation is everything. It's just not *what* you say and *how* you say it; it's also *when* you say it that can make all the difference.

Many years ago, we (Rodney and Michelle) made a bold decision to announce to our families that we would no longer be traveling to

Dallas on Christmas Day like we had been doing each year since we moved to Florida. We wanted our children to wake up on Christmas and experience it in our home so we could establish our own traditions and memories around our Christmas tree. I (Michelle) knew this was going to be a tough sell, and it wouldn't go over very well with my side of the family.

I delegated delivering the dreaded news to Rodney because I knew it would be too awkward and emotional for me to share our intentions with my parents, three sisters, and their families. I also knew the timing would be extremely important to avoid any misunderstanding or dampen the mood over the holidays. Our plan was for Rodney to give them our decision a year in advance, on the last night of our usual Christmastime visit. I'll never forget that evening together with my family at my sister Kim's house. My parents, my sisters and brothers-in-law, our kids, and our nieces and nephews were gathered in my sister's living room. Rodney spoke up and said he had an announcement to make. You could see the curiosity on everyone's faces, as if we were getting ready to make an exciting announcement like we were expecting a baby or maybe moving back to Dallas. When Rodney had everyone's attention, he told them, "Everyone, this is the last Christmas we'll be coming to Dallas."

You could have heard a pin drop. Faces displayed confusion, shock, and disbelief. Then all of a sudden, my youngest sister, Heather, broke out in tears and said, "You mean to tell us that our children will never know your children for the rest of their lives?"

Rodney was suddenly sitting in the hot seat. Everyone glared at him as if he could be executed by a firing squad of harsh looks. After the tears and drama subsided, we finally were able to explain ourselves. We shared our hopes and dreams for our family and our desire to make memories and establish traditions of our own. It was a tough conversation, but it was worth it. We had charted a course for our three children, and we had communicated our vision to my family so they would understand—maybe not agree, but at least understand.

Once the dust settled from our big announcement, one of my brothers-in-law approached Rodney and said, "Bro, that took some guts! I've been wanting to say that for a long time, but I didn't have the courage to do it. I was afraid of being put on the family blacklist . . . like what just happened to you!"

As Rodney learned firsthand from delivering his big "vision talk" to my family, it's vitally important to know your audience and be aware of how each person is wired as you talk through and implement your plans for the future. You will want to clearly share the benefits to each member of the family before you unveil the process. If we move to the process (the actual steps to accomplish the goals) too quickly, we run the risk of creating resistance among those who need their hearts engaged before they can put their hands to the task. John C. Maxwell reminds us that when it comes to leveraging influence, "leaders touch a heart before they ask for a hand."[1]

Presentation is everything. It's not just *what* you say and *how* you say it, it's also *when* you say it that can make all the difference.

—RODNEY AND MICHELLE GAGE

Let us make a recommendation: Early in the conversations about mission and vision, take time to invite your spouse and kids to dream big. This inspires everyone to envision what could be and should be. God made us to dream. Here are some statements that invite more discussion:

- Imagine what it would look like if our marriage (or family) stood for something far greater than ourselves. What do you think that purpose might be?
- Imagine the impact we could have on people in our family, in the neighborhood, at school, and at work. How do you envision people being affected by us?
- Imagine what our marriage (or family) would look like a year from now, in five years, and in ten years if we kept living for this purpose. What do you think we'll need to keep us going?

And as you read this, how do you imagine these conversations going? What excites you about the prospect of engaging the people you love to uncover God's purposes for you and find His path to accomplish them? You need plenty of motivation too!

Focus on where you want to go, not where you have been.

—ZIG ZIGLAR

CRAFTING

So far, we've asked you to think about, pray about, talk about, and write out your family mission and vision. We didn't expect this to take just one talk. It's a process of interacting, careful listening, reframing ideas, listening some more, and finding what inspires each person. But at some point—maybe now—it's time to craft these statements.

Be sure to physically write out your mission and vision statements. Don't let them just hang in the air. Widely diverse sources from the Bible to university studies show the impact of writing out what we want to achieve. About four hundred years before Christ was born, the prophet Habakkuk recorded God's directive:

> Then the LORD answered me and said, "Record the vision and inscribe it on tablets, that the one who reads it may run. For the vision is yet for the appointed time; it hastens toward the goal and it will not fail. Though it tarries, wait for it; for it will certainly come, it will not delay." (Habakkuk 2:2–3 NASB)

Dr. Gail Matthews of the Dominican University of California reports findings from a conditional group study that 76 percent of those who wrote their goals and checked in on those goals weekly with others accomplished them. Matthews states, "My study provides empirical evidence for the effectiveness of three coaching tools: accountability, commitment, and writing down one's goals."[2]

Writing your statements as a couple or family has several benefits:

- It will force you to clarify your purpose and direction.
- It will lead to clear, actionable first steps.
- It will give you motivation to act.
- It will help you say no to good opportunities so you can say yes to the best ones.
- It will help you overcome apathy and resistance.
- It will give you a clear understanding of the progress you make so you can celebrate each step.

Figure out who you are and do it on purpose.

—DOLLY PARTON

ROAD SIGNS

Since finding and fulfilling God's design for your family is a journey, you'll need road signs along the way. Many companies put inspiring quotes in frames to hang in offices and halls. And is there a teenager who doesn't have a poster or screen saver of a band or athlete in the bedroom? We put these up to encourage us and to remind us of what's most important, and I dare say, the things those quotes and posters advertise aren't as important as your mission and vision statements for your marriage and family.

Put your family vision, mission, and purpose statements in visible areas throughout your home so everyone can see them each day. That's just the first step. Refer to them often to reinforce their meaning. Discuss how you may have gotten off track and how you've come back to the path. I suggest you tell your spouse and kids that you want to engage them by talking about the statements on a regular basis. It could be over a pizza or at your favorite burger joint or ice cream parlor or at Saturday morning breakfast—the location is far less important than the intention to have quality conversations. The purpose for talking about the mission and vision often is to keep the "box top" in front of your family at all times.

A friend of ours did this with his wife and high school–aged son. He explained, "Every night for the next month, I want us to talk— just for a few minutes—about our commitment to our purpose." It took some thought and preparation, but for the next week, he led them in discussions of passages from the Bible (like the ones in this book) and questions about how God wants them to live out their purpose in light of pressures like busy schedules, cultural temptations, and relationships with friends. Finally, he asked them to weigh in vulnerably and honestly about how their purpose shaped their responses to victories and defeats, encouragement and criticism.

When the month was over, he said, "When I started, I was pretty sure my wife was on board, but my son . . . I wasn't sure at all. But

I didn't preach to him. I talked about what I was learning about a host of topics, and I asked him what he thought. When I disagreed, I tried really hard to avoid shutting down the conversation. Instead, I said, 'Tell me more about what you're thinking.' It was far better than anything I had imagined! In fact, I look back on those conversations as the launching pad for more meaningful talks about all kinds of issues since then."

What this father did with his son is what we pray will take place in your marriage and family. He decided to stop the drift and take the necessary steps to make the shift.

The purpose for talking about the mission and vision often is to keep the "box top" in front of your family at all times.
—RODNEY AND MICHELLE GAGE

NEHEMIAH PRINCIPLE

There is a great principle in the Bible known as the Nehemiah principle. Nehemiah mobilized a remnant of people to rebuild the walls of Jerusalem, which had been destroyed by previous invasions. Without the protection of the walls, the Jews living in Jerusalem were left vulnerable to other attacks, so Nehemiah led the charge to restore them in just fifty-two days.

At day twenty-six, when the walls reached half their original height, the workers' strength began to give out. They struggled against threats of attack, low morale, and doubt that the wall would actually protect their loved ones. Nehemiah stepped in to rally the builders together, recast vision, and remind them of the greater purpose they were working toward. He posted soldiers at exposed places along the walls and stationed them next to family homes. Then

Nehemiah offered this reassurance to the people: "Don't be afraid of them. Remember the Lord, who is great and awesome, and fight for your families, your sons and your daughters, your wives and your homes" (Nehemiah 4:14).

You can use the Nehemiah principle to refresh your vision every twenty-six days, or maybe it's easier to schedule a refresh conversation with your family once a month. Don't miss this. The distractions and temptations for more upgrades and experiences from our culture never stop. There's a constant pressure to value success, pleasure, and approval more than God and His purposes. It's not that these things are wrong. If they're gifts from God, we can enjoy them and use them as resources. When we have this perspective, success, pleasure, and approval are our servants . . . but they make lousy masters!

How often do you need to hear your spouse say, "I love you"? How often do your kids need to hear, "I'm so proud of you"? If our hearts are truly captured by God's purpose to make a difference in everything we say and do, we'll talk about it all the time! Especially to the people who matter most in our lives. Remember, what you love the most is what you talk about the most. Your spouse and children need to be reminded of the love, acceptance, support, belief, and confidence you have in them. No one ever died from receiving too much encouragement or hope.

There will always be challenges, distractions, and setbacks along the way. However, our love and commitment to each other must be reinforced over and over. You may be in a single family or blended family and currently feel powerless to lead your children or stepchildren in a way they need to go. We (Rodney and Michelle) want you to know that we believe in you and your family and we have no doubt that God has you right where you are for such a time as this. Your sons or daughters or stepsons or stepdaughters need to know that they are loved and God has a great plan and purpose for their life.

LIVE IT OUT

Every new habit takes practice—and plenty of trial and error. As we change (or at least clarify) the direction of our marriages and families, we need to take practical steps. Each step reinforces our commitment to take the next one, and before long, a new set of habits takes shape.

Let us suggest a few steps you might want to take as you make God's mission and vision real in your experience:

1. Start small.

    Reading the Bible gives us wisdom, guidance, encouragement, and hope. Take a few minutes at the beginning of each day to refocus your mind, heart, and perspective on what matters most to help you live with greater intention. We highly recommend something like the *One Year Bible*, or check out the large variety of Bible readings and devotionals on the Bible app called YouVersion. We have a 40-day devotional on YouVersion called "ReThink Life."

    If you want to make prayer more of a priority, invest time to pray every day. I (Rodney) used to hear my dad say, "Much prayer, much power. Little prayer, little power. No prayer, no power!" If you want to speak with more kindness to your spouse and kids, spend five minutes every day writing down what you appreciate about each person. We suggest practicing these small disciplines in the morning to set the tone for your day. It allows you to be proactive instead of reactive with your day and with your loved ones.

2. Keep the vision fresh.

    Over and over again, remind yourself—and those around you—of the benefits of fulfilling your mission and vision. Point to other couples or families you admire, ask about their motivation, and take encouragement from what they do right. One of the best ways to accomplish this is by reading other books, listening to our *Family Shift* podcast, and attending conferences that are designed to strengthen marriage and family relationships. Remember we reap what we sow. Sow into and invest in your marriage and family relationships.

3. Tell others about your commitment.

Your spouse and kids need to know that you're devoted to what you've all committed to be and do. Invite them to ask if you're being faithful to your commitment. Share what you're learning. Let them hold you accountable, and be a model for them.

4. Enjoy the rewards.

You've made this commitment because you believe God will use it and you to make a difference in the lives of others. From the beginning, as you take steps of faith, you'll see God answer your prayers and take you toward your destiny. Enjoy every moment of the journey.

5. Don't give up.

There will be plenty of times when you fall short of your intentions. It's easy to get distracted, forget about or blow off your commitment, or slip back into old habits. We're all going to mess up and fail along the way. When we get lost on a road trip, it doesn't mean we turn around and go back home—and the same is true when you drift from your mission and vision. We just have to identify where we are, revisit where we're trying to go, and get back on the right track that will lead us to our destination.

To make a shift, we must first take strategic steps to turn our initial commitments into established habits. The good news is that it doesn't take long for a new habit to form in our minds, hearts, and behaviors. Don't wait any longer. Identify the steps you want to take . . . and take them!

 THINK ABOUT IT:

1. Describe what motivates (and what demotivates) each person who is part of your mission and vision as a family.
2. How do you need to tailor your communication to inspire each one?
3. Why is it important to "sell" the benefits before unveiling the process?
4. What are a few very practical steps you can take to fulfill your mission and vision?
5. Do you think it's necessary to remind yourself and others to stay on track? Why or why not?
6. What steps will you take today?

 DO IT:

1. Have another conversation or two with your spouse and family about your mission and vision to make both of the statements clear and strong.
2. Write these statements in their (hopefully) final form.
3. Post them in a prominent place in your house. We suggest to get your statement typed, printed, and framed so that it holds a special place on the walls of your home.

STEP 2

HOLD TO CORE VALUES

A SHIFT IN FOCUS

CHAPTER 4

FAMILY IS
A TEAM SPORT

Strengthen Your Family "Team"

If you're going to play together as a team,
you got to care for one another.
You got to love each other.

—VINCE LOMBARDI

My (Michelle's) parents came to Orlando to visit us a few years ago, and we decided to take them canoeing in an original Florida habitat called Wekiwa Springs. We wanted them to see what central Florida looked like before concrete covered so much of it, and we were excited for them to get a close-up look at manatees and alligators.

Our three kids were in a canoe, my parents went together, and Rodney and I jumped in one. A few minutes later, the other two canoes were out of sight, but Rodney and I had barely budged. It wasn't for a lack of trying—but we were paddling in opposite directions! Instead of working with each other, we were working against each other. We kept spinning around and around very slowly; we weren't making any progress. Paddling harder didn't work. We had to find another solution, or we'd still be there today. Finally, we talked about the problem and figured out how to paddle in tandem and catch up with the others. Canoeing requires two things every family needs: strength and synchrony. When we align our efforts with others in the family, wonderful things can happen. Without that alignment, we get stuck and frustrated.

Alignment is essential. In the North, drivers complain of potholes. Down here in central Florida, we laugh at those small holes in the road. We have sinkholes that can swallow cars and whole houses entirely. Potholes, our Northern friends tell us, can cause significant damage to a car, especially to its alignment. But at least the driver still has the car!

Even so, we had a lot of sympathy for our friend who hit a pothole and had serious car damage. When a driver doesn't see the hole in the road and hits it dead on, it can . . . well, I (Rodney) am not really sure what happens in the dark recesses under a car. To find out, I went to the source—the Firestone website. It explains:

> Alignment is a really complex topic covering a variety of terms and a smorgasbord of parts. When your wheels are out of alignment, your tires aren't pointing in the right direction. This will affect your steering and suspension, but more importantly, it could affect your safety and the durability of your tires and all the parts controlling them.[1]

Even a slight misalignment in the tires can cause a car to drift right or left. If your car moves to the right, you'll hit the bumps on the side of the road to warn you to correct your path. But if you drift to the left, you might hit oncoming traffic, with disastrous results.

Even if you don't have a wreck, the misalignment will wear out your tires more quickly and cost more money.

A lot of families have drifted out of alignment. Each person may have different values, or more often, two or more people may form alliances against some others in the family. Each side is sure they're right, so as arguments inevitably happen, differing opinions become more entrenched. Instead of trying to work with each other, they are working against each other.

Psychologists Les and Leslie Parrott are considered two of the nation's leading experts on marriage. In an article called "The Secret of Growing Together," they write:

> An enduring marriage requires possibility thinking, elasticity, and resilience. It needs continual attention and adaptation to grow together. It requires a shift in interests as our partner's interests shift. In other words, to remain good and strong, marriage entails a lifelong project of adjusting and readjusting our attitudes. For this is the only path to finding positive options to our most perplexing circumstances.[2]

No family is beyond hope, but all of us need to follow the Parrotts' advice to "find positive options," no matter how far we've drifted apart.

The furthest distance between two people is misunderstanding.
—RODNEY AND MICHELLE GAGE

Most family psychologists believe that there are four common parenting types: permissive, uninvolved, authoritarian, and authoritative. These styles, though, aren't limited to parents and kids. We see them in marriages, at work, and in friendships:

- *Permissive* spouses and parents have rules, but they don't enforce them. They may yell, but they don't administer the consequences they've promised would be the result of misbehavior. They claim to be loving and forgiving, and they're susceptible to tears and pleas.

- *Uninvolved* spouses and parents provide little, if any, time, attention, instructions, love, or guidance. Some of these people are simply repeating the example they saw in their parents, and others are so overwhelmed by traumatic life events that they have nothing left to give.

- *Authoritarian* spouses and parents are strict and demanding. What matters is obedience, blind obedience. They don't value others' opinions, and they don't connect with their feelings. From the outside, their marriages or families may look very "put together," but they are put together with fear, not love.

- *Authoritative* spouses and parents are servant leaders. They have a sense of intention and purpose, and they lovingly and patiently take the rest of the family with them. They have rules, and they let people experience the consequences of their choices, both good and bad. They invest time and energy to build strong relationships, and they value each person's uniqueness.

BENCHMARKS

In the chart in chapter 2 we looked at the relationship between mission, values, vision, and strategy (page 31). Now it's time to focus on values and ask the question, "What do we care about?" Or another way of asking is, "What are the nonnegotiable qualities our family is committed to live by?" and "What are the intangibles that will set our family apart and foster success for each member of the family?"

Stated values aren't as important as values we live out. In fact, if there's not coherence between what we say is important and how we act, we send a loud and clear message that we're pretenders. That's painful to write, and we're sure it's painful to read, but it's true.

The Bible is a rich treasure trove of what matters to God and, therefore, what should matter to us. Let us share two passages that communicate God's values loudly and clearly. The first is from the book of Jeremiah. Jeremiah was called "the weeping prophet" because God often gave him such painful things to tell people who weren't following God's path. It's human nature to let the culture we live in influence our values and shape our identities, but Jeremiah said there's a better source:

> "Let not the wise boast of their wisdom or the strong boast of their strength or the rich boast of their riches, but let the one who boasts boast about this: that they have the understanding to know me, that I am the LORD, who exercises kindness, justice and righteousness on earth, for in these I delight," declares the LORD. (9:23–24)

What does it mean to boast? A "boast" is what's most important to us. Have you ever thought about what people living in today's culture like to boast about? Their intelligence, their power, their wealth, and their possessions. These values are supreme in the culture around us, and God warns they're common in many of us too.

At the end of the day, what matters most in life is knowing God and making Him known to those around us. We were made by God and for God, and until we understand that fact, life will never make sense. God wants us to place our trust in Him and to align our values with His: kindness, justice, righteousness, and grace. That's what's most important to God, and as we follow Him, these values become most important to us too. Romans 12:2 reminds us to challenge the norm of our culture: "Stop imitating the ideals and opinions of the culture around you, but be inwardly transformed by the Holy Spirit through a total reformation of how you think. This will empower you to discern God's will as you live a beautiful life, satisfying and perfect in his eyes" (TPT).

Does it matter whether we have our culture's values or God's? Isn't it a lot easier just to go with the flow? It may be easier, but it's deadly. All of us have something that's supremely important to us, something that's worth more than anything. That's why the Old English word to describe our stated value of God is *worth-ship*. When anything or anyone is most important, it becomes an object of our devotion; we invest our energy and time into it, and we expect it to make our lives full and meaningful. In his Kenyon College commencement speech, novelist David Foster Wallace warned the students and their parents:

> If you worship money and things—if they are where you tap real meaning in life—then you will never have enough. Never feel you have enough. It's the truth. Worship your own body and beauty and sexual allure and you will always feel ugly. . . . Worship power—you feel weak and afraid, and you will need ever more power over others to keep the fear at bay. Worship your intellect, being seen as smart—you will end up feeling stupid, a fraud, always on the verge of being found out. . . . The insidious thing about these forms of worship is not that they're evil or sinful; it is that they are *unconscious*. They are default-settings.[3]

Money, possessions, intelligence, beauty, and power aren't necessarily wrong, but they'll cause us to drift if they become our highest values. They simply can't give us what we long for. They're our default settings, so, unless something radically reorients our agendas, they stay at the top of our priority lists. Having a real, authentic relationship with God is far better.

A second Scripture passage gives another glimpse of the values God wants us to embrace. King David wrote many of the psalms. Their contents range from the loftiest praise to complaints that God hadn't come through like David had expected. But even when David was discouraged, he kept praying and seeking God. He often described his love for God and his commitment to value what God values. In Psalm 15, he wrote:

> Lord, who dares to dwell with you? Who presumes the privilege of being close to you, living next to you in your shining place of glory? Who are those who daily dwell in the life of the Holy Spirit? They are passionate and whole-hearted, always sincere and always speaking the truth—for their hearts are trustworthy. They refuse to slander or insult others; they'll never listen to gossip or rumors, nor would they ever harm another with their words. They will speak out passionately against evil and evil workers while commending the faithful ones who follow after the truth. They make firm commitments and follow through, even at great cost. They never crush others with exploitation or abuse and they would never be bought with a bribe against the innocent. They will never be shaken; they will stand firm forever. (TPT)

David valued God's truth, so his words reflected truth he had in his heart about God. David valued kindness, so he treated each person according to the Golden Rule. He valued honesty, so he kept his word even when it wasn't pleasant or convenient. And he valued justice, so he cared for the poor and refused to engage in shady business deals.

Let's be honest: We may aspire to these qualities, but none of us has arrived. Even the humblest, most committed, and most mature among us still wrestle with flaws and temptations.

The goal isn't perfection, it's progress.
—RODNEY AND MICHELLE GAGE

God's promised outcome if we practice His values is in the last line of the psalm: We "will never be shaken." No matter what tragedies we endure, and no matter how much chaos is going on around us, we'll have God's promises as an anchor for the soul. We'll have confidence that when everything around us looks out of control, God is still sovereign over it all.

Years ago, I (Rodney) wanted to do something for my son Luke that would mark the significant milestone in his life of transitioning from boyhood to manhood. Luke was turning thirteen, so I reached out to some close friends who had served as key influences in his life, and I also reached out to some of his closest friends. I invited my father-in-law to fly in to Orlando to participate.

I planned a fun and special evening for Luke. We went to the house of a friend who lived in the country. We cooked out, rode four-wheelers, shot guns, and built a big bonfire. Needless to say, it was a night filled with testosterone! As we approached the end of the evening, I invited Luke to sit in a chair in the middle of a circle. I had asked each of the seven men I invited to prepare a two-minute talk about one of our family's seven core values. Each one affirmed Luke and shared the significance of the value. They challenged Luke to not only embrace that virtue but live it out all the days of his life. Then Luke's friends stood up and each gave Luke kind words of affirmation and shared how much they cherished their friendship with him. As we concluded, my father-in-law gave Luke a ring that symbolized the love and legacy of our family. All these moments were truly moving and memorable. Finally, I stood up and read from the Bible:

> Jesus grew in wisdom [mentally] and in stature [physical] and in favor with God [spiritually] and all the people [relationally]. (Luke 2:52 NLT)

> When I was a child, I spoke and thought and reasoned as a child. But when I grew up, I put away childish things. (1 Corinthians 13:11 NLT)

After I read these verses to Luke, I shared this blessing over his life: "May the Lord bless and protect you; may the Lord's face radiate with joy because of you; may he be gracious to you, show you his favor, and give you his peace" (Numbers 6:24 TLB).

I wanted this evening to be a night Luke would never forget. It was important to reinforce the values that would navigate his choices as he entered middle school, then high school, and beyond. Knowing all that he would hear, see, and experience during those critical years, I wanted him to be reminded of our mission, vision, and values as a family. I wanted our values and the life principles spoken over him that night to inspire him and remind him to stand strong during his adolescent years. I also wanted to reassure him that our family values and God's promises would serve as an anchor in his life.

As parents, we have an incredible opportunity and responsibility given to us by God to shape the identities and values of our children.

It doesn't guarantee that they won't fall into temptation or make bad choices as they grow older, but it does give them a spiritual and moral compass to know what is most important and Who the source of truth is for our lives.

THE POWER OF REGRET

Not everyone has had the opportunity to grow up in a family that taught and lived out strong Christian values. Michelle and I realize that the strength and depth of our childhood experiences are rare today. Perhaps the family you grew up in was anything but a loving family. Maybe you had to endure pain, conflicts, and hardships as a child. As a parent, maybe you missed opportunities that you wish you could get back with your kids. The truth is, all of us have made mistakes, and all of us have been wounded. We've all done things that we wish we had never done. All of us have hurt people we care about. And all of us wish we'd done something different in all these situations.

So, to some degree, we're haunted by regret. Regrets are part of our fallen nature—part of being human. In his book *Your Best Year Ever*, Michael Hyatt observes, "The only people with no hope are those with no regrets."[4] If we don't care about anything, our failures won't bother us. But if we care, we'll be aware that we haven't lived up to our standards, and even more, to God's standards.

Not long ago I (Michelle) woke up in the middle of the night with tremendous pain in my shoulder and arm. I thought the pain was a result of sleeping awkwardly. The pain progressively got worse. After several days of discomfort I finally went to the doctor to get evaluated. I underwent a series of X-rays and an MRI, and I even convinced Rodney to purchase a new mattress, but I was still living with pain in my shoulder. The results from my MRI showed that I had something called adhesive capsulitis. It's a condition more commonly referred to as frozen shoulder. It generally takes time and intense physical therapy for the condition to go away—unfortunately, there's no quick fix.

I learned the hard way that pain can serve as a tremendous indicator that something is wrong in our lives, and it can stick with us for some time. As long as we acknowledge our pain and do something about it, we can overcome it. Pain can birth something positive if we'll let it. Let time be your friend and don't rush things—the best things take time. Regret isn't the worst thing in the world. It certainly can crush a person with a sense of worthlessness and helplessness, but if we let it, it can be a powerful fuel for growth. The problem is that we hate the feeling so much we often fail to acknowledge it, and if we don't acknowledge it, regret will eat us alive from the inside out.

Sometimes, however, our regrets aren't that we've hurt someone or turned our backs on God. Instead, we're sorry that we missed a golden opportunity; we didn't take advantage of time we could have spent with someone we love, or we made a financial decision that we thought was a good one but turned out to be bad. Again, our thoughts about these things can weigh us down like a ton of bricks or propel us to make better choices in the future. No matter what has happened in the past, the door of the future is always open to us. It's time to leave regrets behind and create a new beginning. Where you've been or what you've done (or didn't do) doesn't matter. You can start with a clean slate.

WRITE THEM DOWN

If we don't write things down, our convictions easily evaporate into thin air. Starting right now, it's time to define what is important to you. A subset of the family mission is a set of clear values. Here you should answer the question, "What do we care about?" Your answer may be a series of words or phrases that reflect your purpose, and these words could be incorporated in the mission statement.

It's time to write down your values. If you're single, spend some time reflecting on what's most important to you. If you're married, set aside time to discuss the values that are most important to you as a couple and the values that you want to pass along to your children. If you already have kids, let them participate if they're old enough. You can call your list of values whatever you want: your family creed, code, or values. The main thing is to get the list in writing. Leadership expert Craig Groeschel gives us encouragement and a warning: "If everything is important, nothing is important. If you value everything, you don't value anything."[5] He recommends a couple, a family, or a company have no more than ten stated values.

A number of years ago we (Rodney and Michelle) sat down and wrote what we felt was most important to us. This exercise allowed us to be thankful and appreciative for the values taught in our homes growing up. It was a challenge to narrow our list down to less than ten, because we could identify many important things. We went through multiple drafts and finally had a list of values that we agreed were going to be the nonnegotiables for our family. We sat down with our kids and shared what we believed captures God's heart for us and our heart for Him:

GAGE FAMILY CORE VALUES

Honor is our choice.

Loyalty is our commitment.

Excellence is our spirit.

Positivity is our attitude.

Purity is our heart.

Generosity is our way.

These values are far more than words on a page. They serve as guidelines to direct us and guardrails to keep us from running into the ditch. We refer to them when we're making decisions, and they are the background music of our lives. They reinforce our *mission*, why we exist, and our *vision*, where we're going. We can't emphasize enough how incredibly important this exercise is for you and your family. If you don't have kids, this is a great opportunity to establish written values for your marriage. It's a big advantage to start now so that if or when you have children, you'll already have a moral "code" for your kids to live by. Perhaps you already have kids. Regardless of their age and stage, this exercise can be a game changer, but only if you live by the values you outline.

It's one thing to have the values hanging on the wall—
they have to be lived out down the hall.

—RODNEY AND MICHELLE GAGE

Some parents assume they've lost their influence on their teenage children. That's not the case at all. They're still watching, still internalizing the values you're displaying through your words, attitudes, and actions. If you've done a good job imparting strong values to your kids, keep it up. If you've drifted from strong values in the past, as we stated earlier, you don't have to live with guilt or regret. Again, it's never too late to make the shift. We've seen God do amazing things in the lives of families when parents who have been authoritarian, permissive, or uninvolved have trusted God, made a major shift, and learned to love like Jesus loves. Strained marriages can be mended, distance can be bridged, pettiness can be overwhelmed by kindness, and bitterness can be turned into respect and love.

That's what you want, isn't it? We're sure it's the reason you're reading this book. A shift in values may be a minor midcourse correction or it could be monumental. Either way, you can do it. Define your values, write them down, and own them. When it comes to casting vision, clarifying your mission, and identifying your core values as a family, say it, spray it, wheel it, and deal it until everyone in the family feels it!

 THINK ABOUT IT:

1. What signs point to a marriage or family being out of alignment?
2. How would you describe the traits and the impact of parents who are . . .

> . . . permissive?
> . . . uninvolved?
> . . . authoritarian?
> . . . authoritative?

3. Which of the Scripture passages in this chapter most powerfully captures your heart and reflects your values? Explain your answer.
4. What are some specific ways you can make a shift away from the world's values of beauty, intelligence, power, and money?
5. How do you want God to use your stated values in your life, as well as in the lives of your spouse and your children?

DO IT:

Answer and discuss these questions as a family:

1. It will take time to refine your list of values so you wholeheartedly commit to them, but for now, what are the words that describe your values?
2. Where is a place in the house where you can display your values where everybody in the family will see them each day?

CHAPTER 5

RULE BOOKS, PLAYBOOKS, AND THE GOOD BOOK

Build Unshakable Values

The number one influence on a child's life
is not their peers, it's their parents.
—RODNEY GAGE

Matthew Emmons is an American expert marksman. In the 2004 Summer Olympic Games in Athens, Greece, Matthew was on his way to winning his second gold medal. In fact, he was so far ahead of the competition that practically all he had to do to finish first was hit anywhere on the target. Like he always did, Matthew aimed high at twelve o'clock and slowly lowered the barrel of his gun down until he took dead aim at the bull's-eye. He gently pulled the trigger . . . and hit his mark. The crowd cheered, but suddenly, Matthew realized he had aimed at the wrong target! His mistake dropped him from first place to eighth, and he lost out on a treasured gold medal.

Sadly, that is a picture of many people in our culture today. When it comes to life, they're aiming at the wrong target. Many people are driven to work their way to the top of a ladder only to realize their ladder is leaning against the wrong wall. Most people don't know what they believe or why they believe it. Wrong has become right and bad has become good. According to Barna Group, 83 percent of adults are concerned about the "moral condition" of the nation. The report continues:

> Given that 84% of all adults consider themselves to be Christian, they have good reason to worry about the moral state of the country. In fact, many of their own views conflict with the moral teachings of their professed faith. Of the ten moral behaviors evaluated in Barna's study, a majority of Americans believed that each of three activities were "morally acceptable." Those included gambling (61%), co-habitation (60%), and sexual fantasies (59%). Nearly half of the adult population felt that two other behaviors were morally acceptable: having an abortion (45%) and having a sexual relationship with someone of the opposite sex other than their spouse (42%). About one-third of the population gave the stamp of approval to pornography (38%), profanity (36%), drunkenness (35%) and homosexual sex (30%). The activity that garnered the least support was using non-prescription drugs (17%).[1]

These statistics are reminiscent of a time in Israel's history when the nation didn't have a king. There was no leadership or moral authority to give direction and meaning to the people. "In those days there was no king in Israel. People did whatever they felt like doing" (Judges 17:6 MSG). Now, thousands of years later, people in our culture still do whatever they feel like doing.

Barna's report indicates that "the moral perspectives of Americans are likely to continue to deteriorate,"[2] as survey trends reveal more and more adults have been depicting the above activities as morally acceptable. George Barna, who has written over thirty books about faith and cultural trends, says most people sense there's a problem but don't believe they contribute to it:

> This is reflective of a nation where morality is generally defined according to one's feelings. In a postmodern society, where people do not acknowledge any moral absolutes, if a person feels justified in engaging in a specific behavior then they do not make a connection with the immoral nature of that action. Yet, deep inside, they sense that something is wrong in our society. They simply have not been able to put two and two together to recognize their personal liability regarding the moral condition of our nation.[3]

As we can see, our culture and society have drifted from God's moral standard and original plan and purpose for our lives. Rather than submitting to God's leadership and authority, we've chosen to do whatever we feel like doing.

SOURCES OF VALUES

Have you ever stopped to think about what you really believe and why you believe it? Have you thought about what you value and why it is so important to you? More importantly, who influenced you to think like you think and believe what you believe? We didn't decide what's most important in a vacuum. A number of sources have shaped what we believe, what matters most, and who we want to become. The different sources have varied impacts on us as individuals, but every person is affected by each of them in significant ways. Let's look at the most important ones.

Popular culture

Our culture communicates values so powerfully and subtly that we seldom analyze them at all—we just soak them in without a moment's thought. Advertising reminds us of the things we don't have in an attempt to sell us on the things we think we need. Music influences our perspective on love and sex, and fashion is always a step ahead with the trends to be sure that what we wore yesterday is already out of style today. The hidden message in all this is, Whatever you have, it's not enough. We end up buying things we don't need with money we don't have to try and impress people we don't even like. People today are obsessed with happiness, but anxiety and depression are more common than ever. Why? Because the promise of happiness isn't found in bigger and better things.

This fact doesn't prevent us from believing that if we try hard enough, the culture's promises will be fulfilled. We've become malleable consumers who are like kites in the wind, quickly darting wherever the wind blows us.

Unless we're perceptive and persistent in identifying the values we see and hear every day, the culture's values seep into every pore by osmosis.

You can't be an influencer if you're always being influenced.

—LEVI LUSKO

Family background

It's hard to overstate the impact of our experiences as children. Some of us are blessed to have grown up in secure, loving environments where people lived out Biblical principles and moral values. But most of us have encountered something less than that . . . and often much less. Many have endured manipulation; emotional, physical, and sexual abuse; abandonment; or the craziness of living with an addict or alcoholic. Internalized pain and confusion twists the values we've absorbed.

Though the wounds we've experienced range from mild to severe, they have shaped us. Even in healthy families, people lie, they get hurt, and they feel angry, but they also have the heart to resolve these things before they take root in each person's soul. In a family that doesn't communicate love and support and isn't honest about pain endured, people have one goal: survival. They play roles to make life work, avoid pain, and gain some kind of autonomy and control. Some become rescuers who live to fix others' problems—which leads to lots of problems! Others conclude they can't trust anyone, so they withdraw, trying to become invisible and stay safe from being hurt again. Still others have an opposite response to the same conclusion: they don't trust anyone, but to them safety comes from intimidating, demanding, and controlling others with intellectual or physical power.

When couples stand at the altar, very few understand the powerful forces that have shaped the person standing next to them. For years after that moment, people wonder why in the world their spouses think, feel, and act in that peculiar way! When one spouse presses the other to explain, the defendant may respond, "I'm fine," which means, "Don't open Pandora's box of all the pain I've spent my life trying to forget."

In an article for Focus on the Family, Kay and Milan Yerkovich recount their struggle to uncover their pasts and resolve recurring problems. The process enabled them to have a much more loving, honest, and supportive marriage for their future.

For 15 years we did not understand this simple truth: Our marriage problems didn't start in our marriage. There were childhood wounds beneath our most irritating behaviors. . . . A pattern of relating to others was set in motion long before each of us met our spouse. Our childhood experiences and the way our parents related to us have imprinted certain thought patterns and behaviors on us. . . . [But] couples with a secure connection are able to evaluate their strengths and weaknesses, own their contribution to relational difficulties and apologize sincerely when they make mistakes. As you consider how to address your love styles, remember this phrase: "Pick your pain." It's uncomfortable to grow and change; it's painful to remain stuck.[4]

Of course, the dysfunction, values, and beliefs we carry into our marriages are also carried into our relationships with our kids. We may not treat our children exactly the same way our parents treated us. Instead of abusing them, we may smother them with attention and control, which produces its own set of problems for their future.

The point is very clear and often terribly disturbing: the problems we have with our spouses and children are usually the product of the values (good or bad) that were ingrained in us when we were children. These values shaped what we believe about love, security, honesty, denial, respect, kindness, control, money, time, and every other facet of human connections.

Friends

Solomon, one of the wisest men who ever lived, realized friends can provide more support than siblings. He wrote, "There are 'friends' who destroy each other, but a real friend sticks closer than a brother" (Proverbs 18:24 NLT). Those who come from relatively healthy families know how to pick good friends . . . and how to avoid people who have a corrosive influence. (We'll talk more about that in chapter 10.) Those who come from difficult families may not have the discernment to pick good friends but they desperately need them. In their book on the full range of relationships, Christian psychologists Les and Leslie Parrott report the results of several surveys on friendship:

> The quality that tops the list in survey after survey of what people appreciate most about their friends is loyalty. . . . They don't tell your secrets to other people. And they don't desert you, even when you are in trouble. . . .
>
> The famous maxim that "a friend in need is a friend indeed" is not the entire story of loyalty, however. A friend in triumph may be even harder to find. Isn't it easier to be a savior than a cheerleader for our friends? It takes twenty-four-karat loyalty for a friend to soar alongside us when we are flying high rather than to bring us down to earth. Loyal friends not only lend a hand when you're in need; they applaud your successes and cheer you on without envy when you prosper.[5]

What does this have to do with our family values? Quite often, great friends impart the values we didn't see and feel and incorporate when we were children. Even if our parents weren't the best role models, our friends can be . . . but only if we choose the right ones.

Show me your friends and I will show you your future.
—RODNEY AND MICHELLE GAGE

Faith and the Bible

By now we guess you can tell that we hold the Bible in the highest regard. It's a book with the most profound message the universe has ever heard, and it imparts that message to those who understand that reading it consistently is a magnificent treasure trove of wisdom and guidance. Many people are baffled when they begin to read the Bible. What's all that stuff about sacrifices and empires and curses? And if Jesus is full of grace and mercy, what do we do with all the "you shall's?" Great questions. From first to last, the Bible tells us about the love and power of God, our desperate need for His grace, and what it means to put Christ in the center of our lives. Yes, there are lots of commands in the Bible, often called "the Law," but God knows we won't and can't fully obey Him all the time. If our relationship with God was based on *our* faithfulness, we'd be in big trouble. Thankfully, it's based on *His* faithfulness to impart His love, forgiveness, and power.

Our beliefs determine our behavior.
What you believe determines how you live.
—RODNEY GAGE

How we see the Bible affects how we view God, ourselves, our spouses, our kids—and everyone and everything else in our lives. We are spiritually born again only and always by God's grace, a fact that gives us a secure foundation in this life so we don't feel compelled to hide or control people. And His grace softens our hearts so we love more like Jesus, loving not only the lovely but the unlovable (and everybody seems unlovable from time to time!). A life lived by biblical principles and godly values allows us to love better and shine brighter to those around us, especially our family.

One of the core values that we adopted into our "Gage Family Core Values" is "faith," but faith in what? We have tried to help our children understand that faith is believing that God is who He says He is and will do what He has promised He will do, even when we don't understand Him. God sees and thinks differently than we see or think. Learning to see life from God's perspective allows us to make better choices. We love the verse in the Bible that says:

> "My thoughts are nothing like your thoughts," says the LORD. "And my ways are far beyond anything you could imagine. For just as the heavens are higher than the earth, so my ways are higher than your ways and my thoughts higher than your thoughts." (Isaiah 55:8–9 NLT)

As we learn to put our trust in God—and walk by faith rather than sight—God begins to do something inside us. Our faith strengthens and our confidence grows because we know God is faithful and true and He can be trusted no matter what we face in life or what temptations may come our way. Paul assured the Christians in Philippi, "God is working in you, giving you the desire and the power to do what pleases him" (Philippians 2:13 NLT).

TRANSFORMATION

One of the reasons why the virtue of faith is so important to us and serves as the centerpiece, anchor, and foundation to our marriage and family is because we have had a front row seat for watching miracle after miracle in our own lives. These miracles have proven God's faithfulness time and again. In over thirty years of ministry experience, we have also seen countless people—people far from God, people who were spiritually lost, confused, and hopeless by the unfortunate circumstances of their lives—experience radical change. We've seen people who have had everything money could buy and who have achieved the highest levels of success find greater purpose through Christ. We've seen people who have wrecked their own lives through devastating choices find hope, forgiveness, and new beginnings through Christ. We know what we believe and why we believe it because we know that with God all things are possible.

Let us tell you a remarkable transformation story. Freddie was born in a charity ward in Houston, Texas. His father was an alcoholic and a street fighter who loaded and unloaded cargo ships in the Houston Ship Channel, so Freddie's grandparents raised him. They lived in one of the city's roughest ghettos. Because he was always surrounded by alcoholism, violence, and dysfunction as a child, Freddie soon followed in his father's footsteps and became involved in drugs and gang violence. By the age of sixteen, he was a leader of one of Houston's most notorious gangs who found himself in and out of juvenile detention centers during most of his teenage years.

While hanging out with friends in a roller-skating rink one night, a beautiful, petite, dark-haired girl captured Freddie's attention. He introduced himself and learned her name was Barbara. She was an only child whose mother had been married and divorced six times. Barbara spent most of her Friday and Saturday nights at the roller-skating rink with her friends. After only a few dates, Freddie and Barbara decided to get married . . . on Barbara's fifteenth birthday. Freddie was seventeen. They both had to get their parents' written consent before they could get their marriage license.

No one was surprised when, only a few months later, Barbara filed for divorce after she saw the extent of Freddie's involvement in drugs, gangs, and crime. Barbara moved back home, and Freddie soon found himself back in jail.

One night Freddie's father went to the jail to see Freddie. Although Freddie's dad was as tough as they come, he had just attended a church service with a friend and had a "born again" experience with Jesus Christ. After hearing a message of hope and how Christ could change a person's life, Freddie's father made a commitment to Jesus in his heart. He told Freddie about his new conversion and promised to pay Freddie's jail bond for his release. There was just one catch: Freddie had to promise to attend a service at the church his father had attended. Being stuck in jail with no prospects, who wouldn't accept that offer?

Freddie fulfilled his promise and went to the church service the same night as his release. Upon hearing the messages of hope, forgiveness, and reconciliation with God, he responded publicly to the altar call that very night. Little did Freddie know that Barbara was attending the same service. While he was at the altar, Barbara happened to be on the opposite side giving *her* life to Christ too.

This may sound like a contrived story to make a dramatic point to emphasize the importance of making a major shift. And besides, just because two people claim to have given their lives to Christ doesn't always mean they will make significant changes in the way they live. But I (Rodney) can assure you that Freddie and Barbara's story was more dramatic than you can imagine, and it was not at all contrived. I heard the story from their own lips and witnessed their journey of faith with my own eyes because I personally knew Barbara and Freddie as Mom and Dad.

Only God could have orchestrated the events of their early lives to have them both at the same place and same time experience a shift that would completely change their trajectory. Shortly after they committed their lives to Christ, God began to do a miracle work in their relationship. They eventually got back together, and, as the old saying goes, the rest is history.

My parents remained together and shared over sixty-four years of marriage. My father after his conversion sensed God's calling on his life to go into full-time ministry. Over the course of his sixty years of ministry, God used him to win over one million people to Christ with the same message of hope, forgiveness, and reconciliation that changed his life and marriage.

My parents are now together in their eternal home in heaven. Their faith and commitment to teach me and my brothers biblical principles and moral values helped shape who we are today.

NEVER TOO LATE

Let us encourage you to build your house on the right foundation, a foundation built on truth, stability, and an eternal promise. It takes some deep reflecting and asking tough questions, but digging into your past and uncovering what makes you tick is vital to realigning your family and charting a course that allows each one of you to radiate God's values. What beliefs and values have shaped your life? What are you building your life on? If you have children, what beliefs and values are you teaching them? How have your beliefs and values influenced your marriage and family relationships?

In His famous Sermon on the Mount, Jesus addressed some controversial issues that we're still dealing with today. He helped his audience understand two of life's most important questions: *Who* are you living for? and *What* are you living for? Are you living for yourself, or are you living for Christ? Are you living for the temporal things or the eternal things? Jesus gives a powerful word picture:

> Anyone who listens to my teaching and follows it is wise, like a person who builds a house on solid rock. Though the rain comes in torrents and the floodwaters rise and the winds beat against that house, it won't collapse because it is built on bedrock. But anyone who hears my teaching and doesn't obey it is foolish, like a person who builds a house on sand. When the rains and floods come and the winds beat against

that house, it will collapse with a mighty crash. (Matthew 7:24–27 NLT)

Matthew concludes this story with a powerful observation: "When Jesus had finished saying these things, the crowds were amazed at his teaching, for he taught with real authority—quite unlike their teachers of religious law" (vv. 28–29 NLT). Don't take the risks of building your life, marriage, and family on the sands of this culture. Don't allow the corrupt beliefs and values of this world influence the choices you make. You don't have to let your life, marriage, or family crash. Even if you have experienced a "mighty crash" in one way or another from choices you have made or traumatic experiences you have endured, God can help you put your life and family back together. Remember, with God's help, all things are possible. We encourage you to make the shift and start today by building your life and family on the solid, unshakable truth and promises that will stand forever.

As we stated earlier in the chapter, we both were very fortunate to have grown up in Christian homes. But just like He did for my (Rodney's) parents, God can make changes in our lives and situations no matter what or who may have influenced us. If you have children, it is our prayer that you will find hope in what we have shared in this chapter and place your faith in God to help you make whatever shift you need to make to transform your most important relationships. Our prayer is that you will be able to say this about your children one day: "It is the greatest joy of my life to hear that my children are consistently living their lives in the ways of truth!" (3 John verse 4 TPT)

THINK ABOUT IT:

1. What are some of the strongest messages in our culture's advertising, song lyrics, fashion, and sports?
2. How do you think your family background has affected your marriage and your relationship with your children?
3. Who are some friends you admire? What are you learning from them?
4. Is the Bible inspiring or confusing to you? What can you do to learn how to understand and apply the truths of the Bible and allow them to transform your life?
5. How do your values line up with God's values? What can you do as a family to live out these values?
6. Read 2 Timothy 3:16–17. What will you allow to be the source of your beliefs and values?
7. If you have kids read Deuteronomy 6:5–9. How will you begin to influence your children so they know what they believe and why they believe it?

 DO IT:

1. Answer and discuss this question with your spouse: What does 3 John verse 4 mean to you?
2. Commit this scripture to memory and pray it as a blessing over your children.
3. No matter what messages we've absorbed from our culture, our childhood, and our friends, God can enable us to make a shift that changes everything. Put your values in action by writing the changes you want to see become a reality in your marriage and family.

CHAPTER 6

WHAT GETS REWARDED GETS REPEATED

Discover the Benefits of a Values-Driven Culture in Your Home

---

Each day of our lives we make deposits
in the memory banks of our children.

—CHUCK SWINDOLL

A couple of years ago when our daughter Ashlyn came home from college for spring break, we decided to make a day trip to one of our favorite beaches. She was longing to get that sun-kissed tan before she went back to school. Since it was spring break, the beaches were busier than normal. There were thousands of people on the beach the day we chose to go. When we finally found a spot to put our beach chairs out, we were ready to enjoy the sun and relax . . . until we overheard (actually, we couldn't help but hear!) a man not far from us yelling at his son who looked to be about eight years old.

The little boy must have committed some heinous crime for his dad to react with so much anger and frustration.

As we listened and watched using our peripheral vision, we learned that the little boy had gotten sunscreen in his eyes. The poor kid was obviously in pain and discomfort. Rather than quickly rushing to help his son, the father kept growling, "Quit your whining! Big boys don't cry!" We were surprised and quite frankly appalled at what we were witnessing, and other people noticed as well. It was obvious the little boy felt helpless, but the father didn't let up. He threatened his little boy, "If you don't stop crying, I'm going to get a spray bottle of vinegar from the car and squirt it in your mouth!"

I (Rodney) was on the verge of stepping in to address the situation, as were others. We were hoping the father would eventually come to his senses to show some compassion toward his son. As we continued to observe the situation, we began to wonder where the mother was. We thought we had seen her earlier, but she wasn't at the scene. Suddenly, Michelle spotted her near the shore. To our shock, she was taking selfies with a selfie stick. We didn't know if she was a fashion blogger trying to catch the "perfect pose" out on the beach, but obviously she was totally checked out from what was going on with her son and husband.

When the mom finally made her way back to her family, she expressed her frustration and anger at her husband. They went at it, flinging insults and accusations. It was quite a scene! Then the couple quickly gathered their belongings along with their little boy and left. Everyone in our small crowd of beachgoing witnesses seemed shocked at the sequence of events. While driving back home from the beach later that day, we couldn't get that situation out of our minds or off of our hearts.

Since then, we've often thought about that scene at the beach. We can't help but wonder what the atmosphere of that couple's marriage and home must be like. We can't help but wonder what that little boy's future will be. What kind of young man will he become? Will he one day repeat the same dysfunction and destructive behavior his father displayed on the beach to his own children? Who knows? We pray that somehow, some way, that family will make a shift for the good in their home before it's too late.

Every interaction, every word we speak, and every look we have on our face shapes the culture of our family.

—RODNEY AND MICHELLE GAGE

FAMILY CULTURE

We often talk about pop culture, cultural trends in politics, and corporate culture, but every family has its own culture too. Actually, creating a positive family culture has many parallels to a CEO establishing a healthy, productive environment in a company. An article on workplace culture in the *Harvard Business Review* can be applied to the atmosphere spouses create in marriage and parents create for their children. The authors assert that creating a healthy culture is one of a leader's most important jobs:

> For better *and* worse, culture and leadership are inextricably linked. Founders and influential leaders often set new cultures in motion and imprint values and assumptions that persist for decades. Over time an organization's leaders can also shape culture, through both conscious and unconscious actions (sometimes with unintended consequences). The best leaders we have observed are fully aware of the multiple cultures within which they are embedded, can sense when change is required, and can deftly influence the process.

But a culture that builds trust and encourages creativity doesn't happen naturally. Many leaders are too disengaged, and the cultures of their companies suffer. The article continues by explaining,

> Unfortunately, in our experience it is far more common for leaders seeking to build high-performing organizations to be confounded by culture. Indeed, many either let it go unmanaged or relegate it to the HR function, where it becomes a secondary concern for the business. They may lay out detailed, thoughtful plans for strategy and execution, but because they don't understand culture's power and dynamics, their plans go off the rails. As someone once said, culture eats strategy for breakfast.[1]

Does this sound like any families you know? In our years of experience teaching and mentoring couples and families, we've seen many people who are like the CEOs in the article—they have goals, strategies, and efforts, but they "go off the rails" because they make the wrong assumptions about the unspoken but powerful forces at work in their relationships. Couples need to work hard to identify, internalize, and live according to values that promote faith, honesty, love, and the other virtues on the lists made in the previous chapters. Perhaps the best indicator of our values is what we reward.

BECOME A GOLD DIGGER

The late Dale Carnegie was known for telling the story of how gold miners found gold. He explained that several tons of dirt had to be removed before a single ounce of gold could be found. However, the miners didn't go in looking for the dirt; they went in looking for the gold. That's exactly the way families should approach the atmosphere of their relationships. It's easy to point out the flaws, warts, blemishes, and imperfections in relationships, but to create a positive, healthy atmosphere, we need to sift through the dirt; we need to look for the good—the gold—and discard the bad. Like everything else, the more good qualities we look for, encourage, and reward in our marriages and in our children, the more good qualities we find.

THE POWER OF PRAISE

We may have very different personalities and widely varied interests, but there isn't a soul on earth who doesn't long for affirmation. That's the reward that means the most to us. It has the power to change the trajectory of people's lives, especially children who are sponges soaking up the verbal and nonverbal communication of their parents.

In her book *The Power of a Woman's Words*, Sharon Jaynes recalls reading the story of a famous artist who displayed his gifting early in life. One afternoon, when his mother was not home, he found some colored ink, found paper, and decided to draw a picture of his sister, Sally. The carnage in the house was fully complete by the time he finished his sister's portrait. When his mother came in, he saw a stunned look on her face; then she gathered him up in her arms and said, "Why, its Sally!" She told him what an incredible picture he had drawn and what a gift he had, and she kissed him on the forehead. Years later, the painter, Benjamin West, never failed to give credit to that amazing woman. He clearly recognized the significance of his Mom's affirmation: "My mother's kiss made me a painter."[2]

Children need to hear—and be convinced of—three consistent messages: "I love you," "I'm proud of you," and "You're really good at [a particular skill]." The first one communicates affection, the second delight, and the third that we see something special for their future. How often do we need to say these words? As often as our children need to hear them, which is very often, but not so much that the words become stale and inauthentic.

I (Michelle) have talked to parents who assure us, "I give my child plenty of affirmation. I'm doing fine with that." But when I look into the eyes of the son or daughter, I don't see confidence. I see fear. Many of us give mixed messages to our spouse and children. We say, "I love you" one minute, but we scowl and condemn the next. We may think the message of love is good enough, but mixed messages are extremely confusing to any recipient. A wise and mature person can handle mixed messages by confronting the conflicting voices. But the vast majority of people are vulnerable because they're too young to know how to interpret mixed messages or they're too wounded to be strong enough to discount them.

Mixed messages may be the most manipulative kind of communication and cause the most damage because they tap into the twin emotions of hope and fear. Those who hear these voices desperately want the words of love and affirmation, and each one inflames their hope to hear more . . . but they are terrified they'll get harsh criticism (like the man gave to his boy on the beach) or icy cold isolation, which hurts just as much.

You obliterate the rewards of verbalized love, delight, and insight into a person's unique talents when you couple that message with anger, contempt, or disgust. "Yeah," you're probably saying right now, "but what about when the person fails or, worse, is defiant? How should I respond?" Great question.

Some of us interpret the failure of those we love as a catastrophe, and we let them know it. Failure happens to all of us—it's not the end of the world! Reorienting our thinking and values surrounding another person's failure can be a big stepping stone into the future. A study by professor Kyla Haimovitz and her colleague Carol Dweck found that when parents communicate a child's failure is debilitating, often "catastrophizing" the event and blowing it out of proportion, the message has powerfully negative effects on the child. Therefore, the two researchers concluded that when a child fails, parents need to focus on what the child can learn from the experience, not the failure itself. Haimovitz encourages parents to ask their kids, "How can you use this as a jumping-off point?" When parents overreact to failure, children internalize their parents' reaction and assume the parents believe failure is fatal and failure is final. What could have been a powerful learning experience turns into an event that erodes the child's confidence and limits creativity to solve problems next time.[3]

The answer, of course, isn't to be blindly positive all the time. Our kids are in a long process of learning and growing. They need to be taught, nurtured, and sometimes corrected. But when we correct them, we need to stay calm, focus on what they can learn, and communicate confidence they'll do better next time. The dad on the beach could easily have said to his son, "Hey, no problem. I'll help you get the lotion out of your eyes." And the next time they went to the beach, the dad could have said before they got out of the car, "We're going to have a lot of fun today. I love being with you!"

Be the attitude you want to be around.
—TIM DETELLIS

FOUR STAGES

As our children grow, our parenting skills need to keep up. It would be silly to treat a high school student the way we care for a three-year-old, but sadly, some parents haven't made the transition. They still believe they need to tell their almost-adult child what to think, where to go, what to wear and to direct every other daily decision. The goal of parenting is to launch children into adulthood with confidence, values, and the skills to succeed. To accomplish this Herculean feat, we need to gradually and carefully impart more responsibility to our children. And at every age, even long after they've left and begun their own families, they need to keep hearing the three foundational messages: "I love you," "I'm proud of you," and "You're really good at this or that."

We've identified four stages of parenting, and in each, we need to reward the right things, behaviors, and values.

Stage 1: Birth to five years old—tenderhearted supervisor

In the early years, children haven't internalized the ability to make wise decisions—not by a long shot! Our role in this stage is to lovingly supervise them and reinforce good behavior. Proverbs reminds us, "A refusal to correct is a refusal to love; love your children by disciplining them" (13:24 MSG). Discipline is not something we do *to* our children; it is something we do *for* our children. Discipline isn't only correcting children who misbehave; it's also instructing, guiding, and encouraging right choices.

In this stage, we reward obedience.

Stage 2: Six to twelve years old—fitness trainer

In this stage, children are growing physically, emotionally, intellectually, and relationally. It's our role to give them the resources they need to stimulate each of these areas of growth. In stage 1, we gave instructions; here, we ask questions to help them think and find the best solution. Gradually, we see them grow in their confidence and abilities.

In this stage, we reward good choices.

Stage 3: Thirteen to eighteen years old—coach

If we give children plenty of instructions when they're little and lots of resources as they grow, they'll have much of what they need when they get to this stage. Our role here is to coach them, to affirm good decisions, help them learn from failure, and stimulate their creativity.

We stop making so many decisions for them, and we expect them (require them) to make more of their own.

In this stage, we reward growing responsibility and independence.

Stage 4: Over eighteen years old—consultant and friend

When our children leave home for work, the military, or college, we launch them with the hope they'll apply all they've learned since they were babies. But we're not finished. We take on a new role of consultant and, sooner or later, peer and friend. If our children know we respect them, they'll want our input. When that happens, we need to avoid regressing to our role as fitness trainer or coach. We give input but with the freedom for our grown children to make their own decisions. Here, we're letting go of control and trusting that our children will have the wisdom to find success and handle difficulties with calm confidence. We begin to see the legacy of our love and values passed down to their children.

In this stage, we reward values being imparted to the next generation.

> The goal of parenting is to launch children into
> adulthood with confidence, values,
> and the skills to succeed.
> —RODNEY AND MICHELLE GAGE

LIFE IS AN ECHO

Whatever we reward will be repeated. It's a principle of human nature and of the kingdom of God. It's important, though, to look beneath actions to notice, name, and nurture the qualities, values, and characteristics we see. We look under the hood to see the engine of each person's motivation—when they succeed and when they fail. The goal is to focus on affirming and recognizing positive qualities, choices, and behaviors rather than focusing on the negative. In other words, be a good finder. Why is this so important? Because the way we see people is the way we treat them and the way we treat them is the way they often become. I (Rodney) love the story the late Zig Ziglar tells in his famous book *See You at the Top*:

> [There was a] little boy who, in a fit of anger shouted to his mother that he hated her. Then, perhaps fearing punishment, he ran out of the house to the hillside and shouted into the valley, "I hate you, I hate you, I hate you." Back from the valley came the echo, "I hate you, I hate you, I hate you." Somewhat startled, the little boy ran back into the house and told his mother there was a mean little boy in the valley saying he hated him. His mother took him back to the hillside and told him to shout, "I love you, I love you." The little boy did as his mother said and this time he discovered there was a nice little boy in the valley saying, "I love you, I love you."

Ziglar shares a vital lesson that comes straight from the Bible. The Bible teaches us in Galatians 6:7 that we reap what we sow. If we sow consistency in our love and affirmations, our spouses and children will reap those traits. Ziglar concludes the story with the lesson: "Life is an echo. What you send out—comes back. What you sow—you reap. What you give—you get. What you see in others—exists in you."[4] Let's commit to being good finders, to look for the gold not the dirt, and to celebrate and reward the good. You will find that what you reward gets repeated.

A friend told us that when his daughter was in high school, she excelled in technology and entered a district contest. She didn't win, but our friend didn't focus on her failure, didn't berate the judge for being unfair, and didn't say anything about the other contestants. He hugged his daughter and told her, "I'm so proud of you! Through all of your training for this contest, you showed dedication, and you really enjoyed learning. And I saw you encourage the girl sitting next to you. I couldn't be happier right now. There's no telling where this skill may take you."

Another dad had a beautiful daughter. He saw how other attractive high school girls were obsessed with their appearance and fashion. The parents of the other girls reinforced this obsession, but this father wanted to give his daughter a different perspective. He told her, "You're very attractive. Everybody can see that. But there's something far more important than appearance—it's character. I appreciate your heart for God, the way you treat people, the fact that you relate to everybody from little children to old people. You bring joy to every person you meet. Make sure you never lose that. It's priceless." She didn't forget. Today, she has two children of her own, and she's having similar talks with them.

A FRESH START

You may be reading this and thinking, *Rodney and Michelle, you don't get it. You have no idea how badly I've messed up. I've hurt people, and the way I've treated them has caused a lot of damage. I'm not sure it can ever be any different.*

Here's the good news: Today is a new day—you can have a fresh start. It's never too late to impart love, honesty, faith and other values to the people who mean so much to you. But progress isn't cheap. It requires us to let God use His scalpel to open our hearts so He can do surgery on the damaged parts of our lives. When we experience God's healing, we'll be different, and we can treat our families with kindness instead of harshness, love instead of intimidation, and respect instead of disrespect, which fosters fear.

Lauri was raised by a demanding mother who was never satisfied with Lauri's performance. Her mother smiled at people outside the home, but inside the walls, she was a bear. Lauri's father knew better than to poke the bear, so he became passive, a nonfactor in the house. But his lack of attention, affection, and protection left Lauri and her brother vulnerable to their mom's condemnation. To no one's surprise, when Lauri grew up and got married, she treated her two girls the way her mother had treated her. She hated it, but her mother's attitude and actions were deeply ingrained in her. She had never seen another way to relate to children.

When her older daughter was ten and the younger was eight years old, Lauri realized how much she was hurting them, so she got an appointment with a counselor. She had always assured herself that she was a good mother and never needed help from anyone—especially a counselor. But now, she realized she simply couldn't deny the reality that she was harming the souls of her daughters. In counseling, she poured out decades of pent up fear and anger. It was exhausting, and she wanted to quit a thousand times, but she kept going. Gradually, the wounds of the past healed, and Lauri experienced more of God's grace than she'd ever imagined possible. As she grew strong and whole, she apologized to her daughters. She invited them to be completely honest about the pain she had caused them, and together, they healed past hurts, expressed and experienced love, and created a very different atmosphere in their home.

No matter where you've come from and what you've done, it's never too late to take God's hand and start over. One of the most encouraging passages in the Bible is a psalm that shows that God never gives up on us. Asaph, whom King David appointed as a writer, singer, and chief musician, had witnessed much corruption and abuse in the temple by other officials. He was deeply disappointed with the way his life was working out, and he wrote:

Then I realized that my heart was bitter, and I was all torn up inside. I was so foolish and ignorant—I must have seemed like a senseless animal to you. Yet I still belong to you; you hold my right hand. You guide me with your counsel, leading me to a glorious destiny. (Psalm 73:21–24 NLT)

You may be at the point of being so angry and frustrated that you feel like "a senseless animal." Even if you're not there, you probably know someone who is. God's assurance is that we're never out of reach. He still holds our hands, guides us in a better path, and takes us to a place where we experience far more of His love, forgiveness, and power. You can start over.

The goal of parents isn't to ensure our kids get a good education, land a good job, find a spouse, and give us grandchildren. The goal is for our kids to grow wise and strong, living for the values that are far higher and far deeper than anything the world thinks is important. When they internalize God's values, our kids will have an impact on their generation no matter what their career paths look like, and they'll instill these values in their children, leaving a legacy for the generations to come. This can only happen if we reward the right things.

We turn again to Solomon, who wrote this sage advice: "Dedicate your children to God and point them in the way that they should go, and the values they've learned from you will be with them for life" (Proverbs 22:6 TPT). The way you relate to your spouse and kids is pointing them in some direction. Stop the drift, make the shift . . . to change the atmosphere and culture of your home. We can change. We become what we're committed to!

 **THINK ABOUT IT:**

1. Recall the man on the beach. What might have been the underlying cause of his anger and intimidation? Do you have any compassion for him? Why or why not?
2. How would you describe the culture of your family? What would a perceptive outsider say about it?
3. What is the power of affirmation?
4. What attitudes and behaviors did your parents reward when you were a child?
5. In which of the roles in the four stages of parenting do you feel most comfortable? Which one feels most uncomfortable? Why is that?
6. Why is it so important to "look under the hood" and notice, name, and nurture the values you see in your spouse and children?
7. On a scale of zero (none) to ten (off the charts), how much hope do you have that you can learn to reward the right things in the members of your family? What are you doing well now? What needs to change?

 DO IT:

1. Have a conversation with your spouse about the different stages in parenting your kids.
2. When you've identified your current role (tenderhearted supervisor, fitness trainer, coach, or consultant and friend), answer and discuss this question together: What are some things you can do better or differently to fulfill your role in each stage?

STEP 3

IDENTIFY YOUR GPS

A SHIFT IN MOTIVATION

CHAPTER 7

ENVISION THE FUTURE

GPS: *Clarify Your Goals*

We are what we repeatedly do.
Excellence, then, is not an act, but a habit.
—ARISTOTLE

Did we lose you when you read the title of this chapter? Some people love to set goals, but others despise them. Is that too strong a word? Not for those whose stomachs churn whenever anyone talks about nailing down specific goals. Those who have encountered failed attempts in the past when it comes to goals would rather have a root canal with no anesthesia than set more goals. Why such widely varied responses to the idea of establishing goals? There are several reasons.

First, some people are temperamentally wired to be concrete in their thinking. They don't like abstractions. They only feel comfortable with carefully spelled out plans. These are the people who get frustrated when a friend who invites them to do something fun won't agree on an activity or changes plans without any notice. These are the employees who always ask for crystal clear goals, plans, and deadlines. They want to know exactly what's expected and what it will take to succeed. This is the spouse who makes lists (and maybe lists of lists), writes out what to take on a vacation, has an ironclad budget, and has every item of clothing neatly folded or hung. Without a plan, these people feel out of control.

But there are people on the other end of the pendulum— and people in the first group are often married to them! To these people, rules, plans, schedules, deadlines, and clear expectations feel like entrapments. They value freedom of expression and feel comfortable with open-ended concepts. A deadline makes them tense, unless they completely ignore it, which is the way many of them handle deadlines. This is the friend who doesn't care what you do together as long as you're spending time with each other. This is the employee who may be wonderfully talented but drives managers and colleagues crazy by getting off track in meetings and being late with work. This is the spouse who spends without a budget, loves to make spontaneous decisions, and lives for excitement and freedom.

Into this mix, we throw our kids, who may be just as different from one another as their parents.

In the third step of our 5-Step Plan, we're going to look at the guidance system of a family, the GPS: *goals*, *passions*, and how we can respond to *struggles* in ways that help us grow stronger. But first, let me (Rodney) tell you about an experience our family had setting goals.

Michelle and I came to our marriage from very different backgrounds. I'm the youngest of four boys and she's the oldest of four girls. My family was very competitive and risk-taking. Her family was very affectionate and conservative. She's a typical "oldest child" who is conscientious and very responsible. I roll the dice and play things more loosely—you middle or youngest born know what I mean. We may have been very different, but we were partners in a dumb decision early in our marriage.

When we got married, both of us had cars that were paid for. No car payment is what most families long for, right? We wanted a sports car. Michelle drove an old Chevy Camaro (canary yellow) that was falling apart, and I had a Jeep. We decided to sell Michelle's car and trade my Jeep Cherokee for a tiny, two-door Mitsubishi Eclipse Turbo. And we went into debt to get it. Not long after, we realized our error. Our goal of looking cool wasn't as important as the goal of being financially responsible. The problem was that we hadn't yet identified our goals. Chances are, we're not alone in making this mistake.

Let's be real: Virtually every company, large and small, every church, and every other organization invests time, energy, research, and dollars to set goals that give both direction and motivation to everyone involved. But we've noticed that couples and families seldom even have goal-setting on their radar. Our family relationships are the most important ones we have had, have now, and will ever have. It's important to have clear goals that enable us to bring our mission and vision forward with tangible, specific, and measurable steps. We like to call them *faith* goals to live by.

Focused: They must be specific.

Attainable: They must be realistic and practical.

Individual: They must be your goals, not someone else's.

Trackable: You must be able to measure progress.

Heartfelt: Your goals should motivate you and ignite your passion.

SETTING TARGETS

In his book *Your Best Year Ever*, Michael Hyatt identifies ten specific areas to set goals in. Zig Ziglar's "Wheel of Life" focuses on seven areas. However, we propose five targeted areas specific to setting goals for your marriage and family. We envision these areas as limbs on a tree.

When a tree is healthy, it grows organically and bears fruit. In the same way, a healthy family that's rooted in the soil of right beliefs will grow as strong as a mighty oak and withstand the storms and obstacles that inevitably come. To help visualize goal-setting for your family, we developed the Family Goal Tree. It consists of five branches representing five areas of growth for families: spiritual, relational, financial, intellectual, physical. The mission, vision, and values you set in place for your family bring all five "limbs" or components to life.

The Family Goal Tree is a perfect metaphor for a life of growth and strength. Our values are the roots that sink deep in fertile soil to nourish our dreams. The mission and vision statements your family creates serve as the ground, the foundation, the soil your tree will use to grow. Each limb of the tree clarifies and solidifies choices. And as these limbs grow, the whole tree becomes fortified. Like the tree, our families need to be focused on five limbs of growth.

Spiritual

Growing spiritually is not a destination, it's a journey. We are as close to God as we choose to be. Every day, we should strive to sow spiritual seeds of growth so that we can develop deeper roots of our faith. How? Through daily Bible reading, memorizing scriptures, prayer, attending church, serving, sharing our faith with nonbelievers, and doing life with others followers of Christ. We get out of our spiritual life what we put into it. Our daily routines and habits foster spiritual growth and success. Sowing these seeds has a compound effect on our lives, and consistently doing so keeps the soil of our hearts fertile and soft. The by-product is spiritual confidence.

On a scale of one (bad) to ten (great) where would you and each member of your family rate your current relationships with God? What are two or three goals you can put into action to move the needle on your family's spiritual growth?

Relational

As James 4:8 teaches us, when we come close to God, He will come close to us. Our God is a relational God. He made us so He could love us and have a relationship with us. Therefore, the stronger we are spiritually in our relationship with God, the stronger our relationships will be with each other. It's important that we become students of each other's needs, personalities, passions, etc., and nurture those in a way that produces trust, honor, love, and support. When we sow into our relationships we reap the fruit of those relationships. Again, it keeps the soil of our hearts fertile, soft, and open toward each other. Using the same scale as above, from one to ten, how would you rate your current relationships with your spouse and children? What are two or three goals you can put into actions to deepen and strengthen your relationships with each other?

Financial

The Bible teaches us in Matthew 6:21 "Your heart will always pursue what you value as your treasure" (TPT). If making money and having financial security are what you value as your treasures, then these things usually takes priority over everything else. There is nothing wrong with earning and having money. Nor is there anything wrong with financial security. The purpose of setting financial goals is to be prepared for the future. The question is, Who, where, and what are we putting our trust in? Growing financially is about living in freedom rather than bondage. God wants to be first in every area of our lives, including our finances. A good goal to strive for when it comes to growing financially is to give 10 percent, save 10 percent, and live on 80 percent of what you earn.

Alignment with God's plan puts us under the umbrella of His provision and protection, which is the ultimate form of security. As with the previous limbs, when we sow into eternal things, our hearts remain fertile toward the things that matter most. Using the scale of one to ten, how would you rate your current financial state as a family? What are two or three goals you can set as a couple or as a family to help set up your lives for financial success?

Intellectual

The difference between where you are and where you desire to be is what you know. We should always be sowing seeds into our own personal growth. Whether through reading books or articles, listening to podcasts, attending seminars or webinars, getting an additional academic degree, or pursuing more job training, it is important that we keep growing and stretching to reach our God-given potential. We not only need this personally and professionally, but our kids also need to be challenged and inspired to do their best and to become people of excellence. On a scale of one to ten, how would you rate your satisfaction with what you know today? Using the same scale, how motivated are you and your family to pursue new knowledge? What are two or three goals you could put into action that will help you grow from where you are to where you desire to be personally, professionally, and academically?

Physical

Why is this so important? Because we want to be at our best for the people we love the most and to fully enjoy this one and only life we have. Giving our best means having the strength, stamina, and energy to run the race God has called us to run. We set goals for growing physically in our lives to give God and each other our very best as stewards of our bodies. Physical activities are a wonderful way for our families to spend time together, grow closer, and honor God by honoring our bodies. On a scale of one to ten, how would you rate your physical fitness? What are two or three goals you could put into action as an individual, couple, or family that will move the needle to growing stronger and healthier?

People and rubber bands have one thing in common,
they both have to be stretched to be effective
and reach their full potential.
—RODNEY AND MICHELLE GAGE

In each area of growth, we encounter obstacles—reasons to quit or give less than our best. Don't be surprised when you run up against roadblocks and delays. Every good endeavor requires tenacity. Author Chuck Swindoll, says, "The longer I live the more convinced I become that life is 10 percent what happens to you and 90 percent how we respond to it."[1] We can't control what happens to us, but we can choose how we respond to difficult situations and circumstances. In each of these five areas, pursue excellence and never stop growing. Optimism is essential—not blind optimism, but open-eyed confidence that God will give you the wisdom to walk through open doors. The immediate problems can overwhelm us, so we need to keep our eyes on our hopes that God will do magnificent things in us, for us, and through us five to ten years down the road.

We (Rodney and Michelle) have a sign in our kitchen that a friend gifted to us that reminds us of our Family Goal Tree and the five branches of growth. It says, "We all grow in different directions but our roots remain the same."

FOCUSED AND FLEXIBLE

Top executives in business know the importance of setting clear goals. The life of the company depends on thorough planning, clear delegation, and excellence in implementation. However, a chief employee complaint is that team leaders fail to provide this kind of input. When employees have to guess what's important and when something needs to be accomplished, frustration and anger inevitably result, along with lower productivity.

Are families any different? Yes and no. The scope of goal-setting for a couple or a family isn't as comprehensive as a business plan, but it's just as important. Why don't most families have goals? Pain. That's the reason. It's too painful. Those who are naturally bent toward setting goals feel the pain of trying to get everyone in the family on board, and after multiple attempts, the pain seems greater than the benefits. Those on the other end feel misunderstood, disrespected, and even oppressed when someone in the family tries to make them set and accomplish specific goals. That's their version of too much pain and too few benefits.

Does the Bible give us any answer to this dilemma? Yes, lots of answers, and a wonderful balance between the two extremes. The book of Proverbs contains many insights about setting goals. For instance, Solomon explained, "Wise people think before they act; fools don't—and even brag about their foolishness" (13:16 NLT). And his words remind us that our plans aren't the only game in town: "You can make many plans, but the LORD's purpose will prevail" (19:21 NLT).

We also see this blend and balance in the Lord's Prayer. Jesus taught us to pray, "Our Father in heaven, may your name be kept holy. May your Kingdom come soon. May your will be done on earth, as it is in heaven" (Matthew 6:9–10 NLT). Our clear goal should be the prioritization of everything in our lives to bring God's kingdom of kindness, love, forgiveness, truth, and righteousness to our homes, schools, neighborhoods, and jobs. But life often throws us curveballs. In the surprises that happen, God is still working, accomplishing His will through the unexpected blessings and heartaches. We need to be both focused and flexible.

OVERCOMING THE PAIN

Let's face it: all of us feel disappointed or frustrated by people who see goals differently than we do. We've tried to set and live by clear goals . . . or avoid what we perceive as the straitjacket of goals . . . but some people we care about don't see things our way. Usually, the resulting disagreement is just a mild rash, but sometimes, it's the flu! Far too many of us have become defensive, expecting conflict and trying to manipulate and manage our way around the problem.

There's a better way.

We need to focus on the benefits the other person will receive by setting and achieving goals. That's right, *the other person*. If we only think (or primarily think) about what we want, we'll keep butting heads. But if we enter the other person's world, discover what matters most from that perspective, and then craft the process and the plans so the other person sees the benefit, everybody wins. It's not that hard. The loose, creative, fly-by-the-seat-of-your-pants people can realize their spouses need more structure, clear expectations, and at least a ballpark goal for the most important elements in life.

By focusing on the benefits of compromise and moving toward each other, spouses will tap into each other's heartfelt motivations. Instead of being painful, setting goals together can become rewarding, and eventually, both parties can be thrilled that they're working together toward their shared objectives.

When I (Rodney) was in high school, I had a serious motorcycle accident while attempting to race motocross. At the time, I didn't realize the impact it would have on my neck, ultimately causing me to suffer from three herniated discs. Eventually, I developed chronic neck and back pain, and I often found myself in the chiropractor's office. My pain usually was in the upper-middle part of my back between my shoulder blades; however, the first time the doctor gave me an adjustment, he worked on my neck. I argued that my pain was between my shoulder blades, but he explained that I was experiencing "referred pain." I was feeling pain in one area that was actually being caused in another area. I was out of alignment. He gave me an adjustment in my neck, which relieved the pain and discomfort in the upper-middle part of my back.

We (Rodney and Michelle) meet a lot of people who feel pain and discomfort in different areas of their lives—they suffer from struggling marriages, poor health, stress at work, financial problems, etc. One of the things we've learned is that the pain they feel may not actually be the real problem. The pain can be a symptom from another cause. Most of the time, the pain is due to a misalignment with their goals and purpose, and they need to make necessary adjustments. So how do you do that?

A GOAL-SETTING STRATEGY

Let us offer a strategy to help you and your family focus on the benefits of planning and setting goals and find the motivation to accomplish them.

Dream

Don't start with a calendar and a budget sheet. Instead, start with plenty of time to think, dream, and imagine what your family can be. This is second nature to the freethinking people in the family, but the more structured ones need this time just as much. Don't criticize your spouse's ideas. Just talk; let your mind imagine what your relationships might become, what fun times you might have together, what meaningful ways you can serve together, and what it will mean to instill God's values into your children. Some will want to rush through this. Don't! Spend several unhurried times together to let the ideas marinate. You may want to do this first as a couple, but if your children can participate, include them in a second phase of dreaming big dreams. You may have already done some big dreaming when you wrote your family mission and vision.

Set major goals

If you've dreamed together and found common ground, it'll be easy to write down the goals that have surfaced for your marriage and your family. Some people prefer to have one or two major goals in each of the five areas (spiritual, relational, financial, intellectual, physical) on the limbs of the Family Goal Tree. These can be as specific as having dinner three times a week with the whole family, having a weekly date night, saving a particular amount of money, exercising for a certain amount of time and number of days each week, and other attainable goals.

Make sure everyone is involved. If family members aren't allowed to give their input, they probably won't own the goals. You'll need to help the younger children set their goals, but as they get older and have more abilities in thinking and decision-making, encourage them to come up with their own.

Some of the goals for kids won't be on the lists they make. They probably won't be thrilled to make up their beds, pick up their clothes, and do household chores, but these will build character. Sweeten the deal by rewarding them with something they like and enjoy if they reach these goals each week. But make sure they also have goals they're excited about pursuing and reaching.

ESTABLISH PRIORITIES

Unfortunately, most people's lives aren't defined by what's *important* but by what's *urgent*. The tyranny of the urgent gets us out of alignment with the things that matter most in our marriages and family relationships.

Everything worthwhile is uphill.

—JOHN MAXWELL

The reason why worthwhile things are uphill is simply that they don't come easily. We have to fight for them. We have to decide what's important to us and fight to protect those things that will bring us purpose, joy, and fulfillment.

Many of us are already stressed by all the things we're trying to do, so perhaps the first priority is to weed out some things from the schedule. Our closets can be cluttered, but so can our schedules! We recommend you look at your major goals and put them in three categories: now, soon, and later. You may have some huge concerns that need to be addressed right away. Focus on those for a while and get them resolved, and then move to the next things on the list. As you negotiate what belongs in each category, remember to relax, focus on what motivates the other people in your family, be flexible, and compromise.

Of course, make goals age appropriate for your children. Picking up toys every night before bed might be one of a toddler's only goals, but as children grow, you can help them set goals that will build character as well as bring fulfillment and joy to their lives.

Here are some goals we prioritized that can serve as suggestions for you and your family:

1. Plan a weekly family fun night. Keep this sacred.
2. Have dinner together at least three to four nights a week.
3. Have consistent date nights for mom and dad. Keep this sacred.
4. Pray together at meal time and over our children each night.
5. Serve at church or in the community.
6. Give financially to God through your local church.

Post your goals

In his book *Free to Focus* author Michael Hyatt writes, "What gets scheduled gets done."[2] It's important to keep your family's goals in front of you, especially on your calendar. Get everyone involved to post your goals on the refrigerator, make a screensaver, or put sticky notes on a centrally located vision board. If you're working toward an incremental goal like saving money for a bike or a vacation, you can create a "thermometer" and mark each step of progress. At one point, we had a giant plastic Coke bottle that we used to put our spare change in. It was our way of saving up for our summer vacation. The day before we left to go on vacation, we took the bottle to the coin machine at the grocery store to count our savings and convert the coins to cash. Before we had the total, we let each person guess the amount. The money went toward doing fun things on vacation. The kids loved it, and this strategy served as motivation to give and save.

Start small

It's really important to have enough wins that everyone in the family stays motivated. Small successes are more easily achieved and keep the ball rolling toward bigger goals. We recommend having some daily goals (like making the bed or putting dishes away) or at most weekly goals (like mowing the lawn, setting the week's agenda, or meal planning). When people have a sense of accomplishment, they'll be encouraged and strive even more.

Take inventory

It's easy to forget goals and plans when we don't regularly evaluate them. Most of us have had that experience. We started an endeavor with big dreams and clear plans, but over months and years, the initial vision faded to black. Don't let that happen! Create a "time block" or call a "family huddle" at the first of each month to reflect, review, and evaluate your progress. Are you in proper alignment with the things you say are important? If not, make an adjustment so that your life is in proper alignment with your goals, purpose, and priorities. Don't be afraid to shift your goals and priorities to keep each person motivated. In these conversations, don't focus on what wasn't accomplished and goals that weren't met. Camp out in the successes and spend most of your time there. Always come back to the benefits of each goal that keep each person motivated. Duty motivates some, but benefits motivate everybody.

CELEBRATE ALONG THE WAY

Don't wait until you reach a big goal to celebrate. Make a big deal of the steps your family takes on the road to completion and growth. We've already looked at the power of affirmation; look for ways to tell people, "You're making progress! Way to go!" The five most important words we can ever say are, "You did a great job!"

A goal without a plan is just a wish.

—RODNEY AND MICHELLE GAGE

Make goal-setting fun. If setting goals and pursuing them is a grind, the process is doomed from the beginning. Whatever it takes, make it fun. Dream, laugh, and encourage big dreams and small steps forward.

Does all this seem like a mountain too big to climb? We hope not. Yes, it takes time to think, pray, dream, and plan, but it's well worth it. Setting family goals and creating an atmosphere of enthusiasm to reach them is one of the biggest shifts a family can make. Great families don't happen by chance, and they aren't created by magic. It's all about living with grater intention. Setting inspiring goals and making progress toward them stops the drift and motivates the shift.

THINK ABOUT IT:

1. On the spectrum of structured to freewheeling, where does each person in your family fall? Have the differences created tension in the past around goals and steps to reach them? How so?

2. What saps your energy and enthusiasm about setting goals at work, in school, or in your family? What excites you?

3. Pick one person in your family who is different from you in how you set goals. Enter that person's world and describe what motivates them. What benefits of setting goals and reaching them rev that person's engine?

4. Why is starting out with imagination so important?

5. What are some specific, age-appropriate goals for your children?

6. How do you plan to go through a process of crafting, pursuing, and staying on track with your family's goals? What difference will it make for you and for them?

 DO IT:

1. Use the worksheet on the next two pages to craft your goals.

2. In the next few days, schedule a time to talk with your spouse and imagine what God wants to do in and through your family. Then, when you have identified some hopes and dreams, carve out time in the next week to go through the worksheet. The goal isn't to complete it, but to let it represent your hearts' desires to honor God and create an environment in which each person soars!

FAMILY GOALS

REVIEW

What is the mission of your family?

_____

_____

What are your family's values?

_____

_____

What is your vision of the way God will use your family to make an impact?

_____

_____

LONG-TERM

In each of these areas, write all the goals you want to achieve in the next one to three years. (You'll need additional paper.)

Spiritual

_____

Relational

_____

Financial

_____

Intellectual

_____

Physical

_____

FOCUSED AND SOON

Now, identify one or two specific, measurable goals you want to focus on in each area:

Spiritual

_____

Relational

_____

Financial

_____

Intellectual

_____

Physical

_____

What will be the benefits of reaching these goals?

_____

_____

When will you take the first step for each of them?

_____

_____

CHAPTER 8

DO WHAT COMES NATURALLY

GPS: *Pursue Your Passions*

A great leader's courage to fulfill his vision
comes from passion, not position.

—JOHN C. MAXWELL

If we'll let them, our biggest struggles can shift our priorities and refine our direction. When our daughter Ashlyn was fourteen, she developed chronic hives that wouldn't go away. The dermatologist gave her strong medicine, but it didn't help much. We tried other doctors and did whatever they recommended. We took out all of our carpets to eliminate dust, and we became detectives to expose any kind of irritant to her skin. The medicines had side effects of drowsiness, making it difficult for her to concentrate in school. The itching, pain, and sleepiness made life very hard for our little girl. Finally, after a long year, the hives began to subside.

Through all of this, Ashlyn kept a positive attitude. In fact, she went out for the high school tennis team. Though she was only a freshman, she made varsity. By the time she graduated, she was the top player on the team, and she won academic honors. Her experience suffering with the hives gave her compassion for others who struggle with health problems, so much so that at the time of our writing this book she is currently pursuing a degree in medicine with a goal to get her master's and become a physician's assistant. She's a wonderful example of someone whose passion came out of persevering through pain and problems.

Our deepest desires can consume every waking moment, thrill us, and energize us to accomplish great things, or they can terrify us and cause us to wilt under the pressure of facing success or failure. In other words, our passions can rule us, inspire us, or shackle us.

We've explored some deep questions in this book so far: What are we living for? Who are we becoming? Why do we get up each day? What are the values that shape our lives and our families? And how do we get where we want to go? We've learned that having a mission and vision statement and creating values help us clarify and answer these important questions. Now, we can look closer at the engine of our lives: our passion to fulfill our highest aspirations.

Passion isn't just emotion. It's more than that. Having passion is your drive, determination, expectation, and joy in taking each step forward toward something (a goal, dream, place in life, etc.). Far too many of us have small ambitions that don't ignite our passions. And far too often, our ambitions are disconnected from our relationship with God.

He wants our relationships with one another to mirror the spirit He gives each of us individually. In the last chapter, we looked at the importance of setting goals in each of the five branches of the Family Goal Tree. Those goals go far beyond superficial pursuits of wealth, beauty, pleasure, and power. If God gives us those things, we can use them for bigger purposes. Our greatest ambition should be to know God and make Him known through our successes and in our marriage and family relationships.

Your purpose guides you, but your passion drives you.
—MICHELLE GAGE

THE TRUTH ABOUT AMBITION

We often think of "ambition" as a negative term, because we assume it implies selfishness. It often does, but not always—the rightness or wrongness of ambition is in its aim. Paul's second letter to the Christians in Corinth explains that we need to have an eternal perspective and realize this life isn't all there is. Someday as believers we'll be with Christ face-to-face. Our true eternal home is with Him. This assurance gives us hope and clarifies our goals each and every day. Paul wrote, "Therefore we also have as our ambition, whether at home or absent, to be pleasing to Him" (5:9 NASB). Ambition to please God is good, right, and noble.

Does it please God when we have relationships with our spouses and children that affirm them, protect them, and inspire them to become strong, healthy, creative people? Of course it does! Does it please God when we enjoy one another and resolve disagreements? You bet. Does it please Him when we give generously and work together to serve people who are disadvantaged? Yes. These are just a taste of the many ambitions that we want to encourage and model as spouses and parents.

The most important commandant in the Bible is called the Great

Commandment. We love how The Message translation describes it: "Love the Lord God with all your passion and prayer and intelligence and energy" (Mark 12:30).

God is a passionate God—He feels things deeply. Since God created us in His image, we are passionate people. He not only wants us to love Him passionately, but He also wants us to live our lives full of passion—fully alive. In Romans 12:11 Paul wrote, "Never be lacking in zeal, but *keep* your spiritual fervor, serving the Lord." Notice my added emphasis on the word "keep." That tells us that passion is something we can lose if we're not careful. We have to work at keeping our passion fully alive because if we don't, we can lose our passion for the Lord and our passion for life.

As all of us know, life can beat the passion right out of us. Our schedules may be full, but our lives can be empty.

When our lives become overcrowded, how do we restore and rejuvenate our passion?

One of our favorite stories in the Bible is about some men who desperately wanted to see their paralyzed friend healed. We (Rodney and Michelle) love this story because of the men's determination and persistence to get their friend to Jesus. You might wonder, *What does this story have to do with restoring our passion for our marriage and family?* These men faced what we all face—problems and setbacks. They carried their friend on a mat but "could not find a way to [get him to Jesus] because of the crowd" (Luke 5:19).

A crowded life will rob us of joy and passion. The worst thing about a crowded life is that it keeps us from being close to Christ. We know because we've experienced it. You may have heard someone say that the word *busy* stands for "being under Satan's yoke." The enemy of our souls wants to get us so busy that we don't have time or energy for the people who matter most in our lives, let alone God. Like we mentioned in the introduction, if we don't check-in with God, our spouses, and our children on a regular basis spiritually, relationally, and emotionally, we will find ourselves drifting further apart until we "check out." Let us share with you five things we can all do to keep our passion alive.

Do something drastic

In our book *ReThink Life*, I (Rodney) tell the story of when several staff members challenged me to go skydiving. I can't stand heights, so jumping out of an airplane seemed outright crazy! While I consider myself a risk-taker, taking that kind of risk was something I definitely never thought I would do. However, I've also learned to never say *never*. Reluctantly, I agreed to this insanity. Jubilantly, my friends arranged all the details.

Needless to say, I didn't sleep much the night before our jump. Tossing and turning all night, I wondered if it would be my last night to live. Morning came too soon. Bright and early, my eager friends arrived to drive me to the private airport.

We sat through a short orientation. We watched a video about skydiving, received directions, and went over the risks involved. After signing our lives away, we put on our gear, met our instructors, and received a few tips. Then my friends and I boarded the airplane for our jump. I'll never forget taxiing down the runway, taking off, and having reality hit me that I was actually getting ready to jump out of an airplane at thirteen thousand feet and a speed of over one hundred miles per hour . . . strapped to a guy a didn't know. I was freaking out!

My instructor told me that when the red light turned green, it was "show time." I prayed the green light bulb would be burned out so we'd have to abort the jump as my instructor latched his tandem harness to mine. Suddenly the light turned green and someone opened the side door. I felt the powerful rush of wind; the deafening noise of the plane engine filled the cabin. We worked our way to the door. On the count of three I did something I never thought I would ever do: I jumped!

I'll never forget the rush of that moment, the way my jump-suit flapped as I plummeted toward earth. After a few moments of the craziness of falling mixed with the euphoria of floating in the air, my instructor pulled the ripcord. In an instant, we went from the penetrating noise of the rushing wind to the total tranquility of being suspended by a parachute thousands of feet in the air. Floating above the clouds was one of the most incredible experiences of my life.

Sometimes we have to do something drastic to get above the noise and craziness of life. We're not implying that you need to jump out of a plane! We just need to do something drastic enough to break up the mundane routines of life. New experiences stimulate our creativity. If we don't have them, we'll lose our passion and purpose for living. Our mission, vision, and values for our marriage and family can get lost.

The pressures of this world can be overwhelming at times, but when we're tethered to God and direct our attention toward His plans and purposes for our lives, everything comes into focus. Life takes on new meaning—we get our fire and passion back. That's why we have to live in tandem with our Creator who wants to navigate our lives. Like my skydiving instructor, God will help us land in the bull's-eye of His targeted drop zone if we let Him.

The men in Luke's story who couldn't get their friend to Jesus because of the crowd decided to do something drastic: "They went up on the roof and lowered him on his mat through the tiles into the middle of the crowd, right in front of Jesus" (v. 19). They knew this might be their last chance to get their friend healed by Jesus, so they took the necessary actions to deal with the problems and remove the obstacles standing in the way. If you want to restore the passion in your marriage and family relationships, stop and ask yourself this clarifying question: *If I knew I had one month to live, how would I live my life?*

This question helps us realize very quickly what's most important and who is most important in our lives. We encourage you to remove the obstacles in your life that are competing for your passion for God and your vision for your marriage and family. Are you spending too much time at work? Are you bringing work home that is distracting from prime family time? Do your kids need to be in so many activities? Which ones can they live without? What about social media? Are you spending more time on Facebook than you are in God's Book? If we're not careful, all the distractions in life can rob us of the things that matter most—our loved ones.

Expect the unexpected

Have you ever noticed that you can make plans but things don't always go as planned? Leadership expert Craig Groeschel observes, "Sometimes the biggest blessings in life are on the other side of opposition."[1]

The men with the paralyzed friend knew where Jesus was going to be and when He was going to be there. However, they weren't expecting such a huge crowd. Instead of giving up and getting discouraged, they got creative. They lowered their friend in front of Jesus—a very unexpected move. "When Jesus saw their faith, he said, 'Friend, your sins are forgiven'" (v. 20).

Because God is unpredictable, we have to allow Him to interrupt our lives—we have to expect the unexpected and know that God has a way of getting our attention when we begin to lose our passion and focus for what matters most. Nothing will rob us of our passion quicker than the unexpected challenges and setbacks we encounter relationally, financially, physically, emotionally, mentally, and spiritually. Remember the warning signs of drift in the opening chapter? Disappointment, Regret, Isolation, Frustration, and Tension—all of these are symptoms of a root problem of drifting from our most loved ones and the One who loves us all.

Create "God space"

Did you notice where the men in Luke's story lowered their friend? In the middle of the crowd, in front of Jesus—the main attraction. They created space that wasn't there before. We have to do the same thing in our busy lives: We have to create space for what's important—time with God, our spouses, and our children. Nothing is more important than those relationships. The Bible teaches that when we lose our passion, we need to do three things. First, we need to remember the height from which we have fallen. Second, we must repent by admitting to God that we've drifted. And third, repeat. We need to go back and do the things we need to do to live with greater intention.

Keep a constant reminder

Jesus said to the paralyzed man, "I tell you, get up, take your mat and go home." Then the man immediately "stood up in front of them, took what he had been lying on and went home praising God" (vv. 24, 25). Why did Jesus tell the man to take his mat and go home? We believe it was to remind him of the miracle of healing and the new start God was giving him.

On a trip when we visited our family in Dallas, we got together at Michelle's sister's house for dinner and an evening of fun, and she introduced us to a fascinating concept. She had purchased a Maker Kit from myintent.org. The kit challenges you to identify "one word" that best describes your intent. It could be a word that describes a virtue, a challenge you want to overcome, what you're most passionate about, or your highest hopes. The goal is to capture your intent and keep it visible to serve as a constant reminder.

I (Rodney) chose the word *shift*. I engraved it in capital letters on a token, which I now wear on a chain around my neck. How about you? What would your word be? What's your intent? What do you want to see happen in your life, career, marriage, family, health, and so on? The bigger question may be: What shifts do you need to make to remove the obstacles that are robbing you of your passion? Whatever your word of intent, make a keepsake to remind yourself of it daily.

Align with divine design

Our passion isn't an abstract thing. God has filled us with the desire to strive for something greater than ourselves. The word *enthusiasm* is a combination of two Greek words that mean "God within." Passion that is directed by God comes from within, implanted by the Holy Spirit and nurtured by reading our Bibles, receiving encouragement from other believers, and experiencing life as Jesus's followers. In the classic movie *Chariots of Fire*, Eric Liddell is a Scottish man training for the hundred-meter race in the 1924 Olympic Games. His sister believes he needs to give up his dream of running in the games and leave to be a missionary in China. In a poignant conversation, she tries again to convince him, but he explains that running isn't a chore; it's a spiritual experience that delights God. Eric tells her, "When I run, I feel His pleasure."

When do you feel God's pleasure? What do you enjoy doing? Where do you see the hand of God moving you and using you? Our talents and desires aren't the product of random events and biology. God has had His hand in every aspect of our lives, including our passions. Ephesians 2:8–10 connects the dots between the grace of God, our calling, and our passions:

> God saved you by his grace when you believed. And you can't take credit for this; it is a gift from God. Salvation is not a reward for the good things we have done, so none of us can boast about it. For we are God's masterpiece. He has created us anew in Christ Jesus, so we can do the good things he planned for us long ago. (NLT)

Did you get that? You're God's work of art—a masterpiece of His creation! You are designed for something far greater and more meaningful than the temporal things of this life. You were made to make an eternal difference. When our goals align with God's heart and we allow gratitude and desire to unleash our passions, we operate in our "sweet spot" of motivation.

Your career is what you get paid for
but your calling is what you were made for.
—RODNEY AND MICHELLE GAGE

Our experiences confirm (or challenge) our goals and passions. For instance, when we (Rodney and Michelle) sit down with couples to help them find and follow God's will for their families, all the lights on our souls' dashboards flash green. We love to see them understand what God wants to do in them and in the lives of each of their children.

We encourage young people to try lots of avenues to explore interests. Experimentation gives them valuable experience, eliminates some options, and focuses them on a few. As we get older, we probably have an idea of what rings our bells, gives us great joy, and makes a difference in the lives of others. But it's never too late to make a switch. Plenty of people who have been in a career or pursued interests for decades find the courage to go in a different direction.

PASSION AND PERSONALITY

There are over seven billion people on the planet today, and all of us are as unique as snowflakes, each with particular talents, desires, and experiences. We aren't the chance products of random connections of molecules. God skillfully crafted each of us. David's beautiful psalm praises God for this truth:

> You made all the delicate, inner parts of my body and knit me together in my mother's womb. Thank you for making me so wonderfully complex! Your workmanship is marvelous—how well I know it. You watched me as I was being formed in utter seclusion, as I was woven together in the dark of the womb. You saw me before I was born. Every day of my life was recorded in your book. Every moment was laid out before a single day had passed. (Psalm 139:13–16 NLT)

Since the time of the ancient Greeks, philosophers have identified personality traits and, more important, groups of traits that shape people's desires, pursuits, and responses. For instance, being with a group of people energizes some of us. That's where we come alive! But being in the same group causes others to feel drained; they need to be alone to recharge their emotional batteries. Some of us gravitate toward accomplishing tasks by discipline and detail, and others want to accomplish tasks by involving people. Some are concrete thinkers who see everything in black and white, but others think abstractly and see the complexity in every situation. Some value safety very highly, and others thrive on taking risks. There are many different inventories that help people identify their personality types.

We can eagerly recommend a number of inventories, such as the DISC, Myers-Briggs Type Indicator (MBTI), StrengthsFinder, Enneagram, and others. We want to introduce you to a personality profile developed by our church. It identifies five basic personality types. You will have fun with these within your family. You may even start referring to members of the family by their unique "avatar." See if one of these sounds familiar:

NINJA	You are procedural, task oriented, and a detail lover. You love being as thorough as possible and would rather be behind the scenes than in a crowd. People may never see the NINJA, but they know you were there by the trail of completion left behind you!
MASTERMIND	You are inspirational, motivating, and a team builder. You can see the big picture vision and rally everyone behind it. You love seeing people come together to accomplish a common goal. If you see a great team, you can bet there is a MASTERMIND behind it all!
TRAILBLAZER	You show ownership, initiative, and you are independent. You can tackle just about anything and love to figure out how to do things better. The TRAILBLAZER loves a challenge and will rise to it without fail every time!
GUARDIAN	You are a protector, a cultivator, and you are compassionate. You watch out for the people around you and take care of their every need. The guardian is no wimp though; just try to hurt those close to a GUARDIAN and you'll get your behind kicked!
SOCIAL GENIUS	You are outgoing, friendly, and you are a networker. You love chatting it up with everybody and naturally make people feel at ease around you. Every time I'm with the SOCIAL GENIUS I feel great!"

None of the personality types are better than the others. They all have strengths, and they all have deficiencies. We've seen four specific benefits of using these inventories:[2]

1. You'll understand why you relate to others easily or with difficulty.

    One of the main benefits of these inventories is that we get to look in a mirror and see ourselves more objectively. If we think we have a particular trait, the inventory and analysis may confirm our suspicion or give us something else to consider. These tools also give us plenty of opportunities to talk to our spouses, kids, coworkers, and friends about our interactions with them.

    We need to be careful to avoid pigeonholing people with labels, but labels can help us see people through clearer lenses. For instance, if you're an introvert and your spouse is and extrovert, you feel very different at parties, and how you feel when you're alone is quite opposite. Understanding this opens doors to communication, patience, kindness, and affection.

2. You'll understand why you respond to situations the way you do.

    Some of us feel guilty that we need to take more time to make decisions than others . . . while some live spontaneously without guilt but may regret decisions later. When both types of people understand their bent, they'll realize one type isn't tragically flawed and the other supremely virtuous—they're just different in the way they process information and make decisions. Quite often, when a couple or team discusses their analysis, they exclaim, "No wonder you responded to me like that!"

3. You can position yourself to live out your passions and accomplish your purpose.

We don't use a hammer when we need to drive a screw into the wall, and we don't insist on using a car when we're trying to cross the ocean to France. But some of us are square pegs trying desperately to fit into the round holes our parents or others have told us are our only option. God didn't create us to all be the same, and one of the adventures of life is discerning where we fit best.

4. You'll be more understanding and patient when people can't do what you can do.

One of the most common problems in marriages is that, for spouses who were initially attracted to each other's differences, over time (sometimes not much time!) the wonder turns into disdain. Don't expect your math-challenged partner to do complicated mental calculations. Give your spouse a break . . . and a calculator. And don't demand that your other half make decisions with only a small amount of information when that's not a mode the other person feels comfortable operating in—if you're lucky, your spouse won't bring up all the times your quick decisions bombed!

You'll find the *Family Shift* Avatar Personality Test online on our website at www.FamilyShift.com and share your results with the Family Shift community. Use this test or another one you and those you love want to use together and dive into fun and meaningful discussions about why you think differently, make decisions in different ways, are energized by different things, and respond to conflict in different ways. What does all this have to do with passion? Quite a lot. A passion killer is feeling misunderstood, and when we feel that way long enough, we're flooded with self-doubt—and that's not a recipe for a full, purposeful life!

> Working hard for something we don't care about
> is called stress. Working hard for something
> we love is called passion.
> —RODNEY AND MICHELLE GAGE

God has told us that we're His masterpieces, and He promises to uniquely use each of us to accomplish what only we can do—for Him, for His purposes, and for the people around us. Discover who you are, what you are designed to be and do, and then do it with all your heart.

 THINK ABOUT IT:

1. When and how have you seen passion rule people, inspire people, and shackle people?
2. Before you read this chapter, how would you have defined "ambition"? What makes ambition good, right, and noble? What makes it unhealthy or bad?
3. How have you seen ambition wreck someone's life? (No names, please!) Who do you know who is a good example of ambition focused on God's goals?
4. Do you believe you're God's masterpiece? Why or why not?
5. Take some time to look over the personality profiles in this chapter. Which one best reflects your design? How will these

profiles help you, your spouse, and your kids understand each other more deeply?

6. What are the benefits you anticipate as you talk to your spouse and family about their personalities?

 DO IT:

1. Have each person (who is old enough) take the *Family Shift* Avatar Personality Test (or another one if you prefer), and then sit down to discuss what you've uncovered. Make sure the conversation is encouraging!

CHAPTER 9

TOUGHEN UP

Grow Stronger through Your Struggles

Your capacity for pain will determine
your potential for growth.

—BRIAN HOUSTON

There are three kinds of people: those who are coming out of a difficult time, those who are in the middle of one right now, and those who will face difficulties in the future. If you don't have problems, you don't have a pulse. We all go through struggles.

THE STRUGGLE IS REAL

When our son Luke was seven years old, he faced a medical crisis. Like most families with children, we had a very busy schedule. Our son's schedule alone kept us hopping. We took Luke to ball practice several nights a week and watched him play games on Saturday mornings. In the spring of that year, Luke began to complain of pain in his leg and knee. Because a ball had hit him during one of his practices, we thought he must have broken something, but X-rays revealed no broken bones. Still, he continued to experience pain and began to limp. Doctors wrote it off as "growing pains," but we weren't convinced. After a few months had passed, his limp became more severe, and the pain didn't go away.

A friend who is an orthopedist told us to bring Luke to his house one evening so he could take a look at his leg. After examining Luke, the doctor told us he had a hunch about the diagnosis but would need an MRI to confirm it. When he saw the MRI of Luke's hip, our orthopedist friend confirmed that Luke had a rare hip disease called Perthes, in which the ball of the femur slowly dies. If left untreated, the ball can completely crush under the person's weight, causing major problems for a lifetime.

After much research, we found a world-renowned specialist in Perthes whose office was about an hour and a half away from our home. We immediately made an appointment, but we weren't prepared for the news we heard. The doctor felt that the best form of treatment for Luke wasn't traditional surgery or leg braces. He recommended Luke be placed in a wheelchair for two to four years. There would be no running, jumping, or playing any sports. Needless to say, our world was turned upside down.

I (Michelle) remember walking out of the hospital that day pushing Luke in a wheelchair and trying to hold back tears as I saw other crippled children in their wheelchairs. I was sure we would never see the world the same again. We were heartbroken that Luke would be immobilized during some of the most active years of his life. Gradually, we began to realize that God had a greater plan for our son and for our family. Even though we didn't understand this plan at the time, we knew God was ultimately in control.

For nearly three years, Luke was in a wheelchair. Over the course of those years, many people told us that Luke's life was an inspiration to them as they went through their own personal struggles and challenges. Today, thanks to answered prayer and God's healing, Luke is out of his wheelchair and completely healed, but his healing is only part of the story. Luke has a clearer, deeper perspective about life now because of what he went through during those years. He sees difficult situations and physically challenged individuals with a different set of eyes. Our whole family learned from this experience. It forced us to stop the drift into rampant pessimism and shift our focus on what's most important. We learned that God wants to use our struggles to fulfill His greater purposes—to use them for our benefit and the benefit of others.

We can't control what happens to us, but we can choose how we respond to difficult situations. Keeping the right perspective in the midst of our struggles is the key to overcoming our problems.

We've often shared a particular passage of Scripture with people who face difficulties. James the half brother of Jesus began his letter to Christians very abruptly . . . and quite surprisingly. He wrote, "Consider it pure joy, my brothers and sisters, whenever you face trials of many kinds" (James 1:2).

How would you like to get an email from a friend with a subject line that reads: "Got problems?" and when you click to open it, the first line says, "Just be happy!" I don't know about you, but when I'm facing struggles, the last thing I want to hear is encouragement to be happy in my pain! My first impression is to say, "How insensitive! How in the world do you expect me to be happy when you don't understand my situation?"

Thankfully, the sentence doesn't stop there. In full, it reads, "Consider it pure joy, my brothers and sisters, whenever you face trials of many kinds, because you know that the testing of your faith produces perseverance" (vv. 2–3). The key to this response is "because you know." What, then, do we need to know to respond to difficulties with faith, confidence, and even joy?

Life will either grind you down or polish you up. . . .
It all depends on what you're made of.

—ZIG ZIGLAR

FOUR "FACTS OF LIFE"

1. Struggles are inevitable.

It's not a matter of *if* but *when* we'll face struggles. We may struggle with our health, finances, marriages, kids, jobs, or many other things. You name it, we face it. James 1:2 doesn't say, "Consider it pure joy, my brothers and sisters, *if* you face trials" but "whenever." Count on it—you're going to have struggles. Jesus told His followers, "In this world you will have trouble" (John 16:33). And the apostle Peter wrote, "Do not be surprised at the fiery ordeal that has come on you to test you" (1 Peter 4:12). Problems aren't an elective class that we don't have to take. They're a required course. You don't get out of them by saying you don't want them. No one is exempt!

2. Struggles are unpredictable.

Our oldest daughter, Becca, is a singer and worship leader. During her first two years in college, she had the opportunity to travel with a worship team and lead worship with the Liberty Worship Collective. This team leads one of the largest college worship gatherings in the world.

As a vocalist, your voice is your most important instrument. At one point, Becca began to notice she was struggling with her voice. It was becoming raspy and hoarse, and she had difficulty hitting certain notes. Soon, others noticed too. She went to several doctors. At first they thought she might have strep throat or mono; however, she didn't have the normal symptoms that come with those illnesses. Months went by and her condition worsened.

When she came home during her Christmas break, she wasn't herself. One evening, as we were talking about her situation, she blurted out with tears coming down her face, "I don't know what's going on with me." She felt deeply discouraged. After multiple misdiagnoses, we were finally able to get her in to an ear, nose, and throat specialist who works with some of the top singers in the country. He pinpointed her problem: she had a yeast infection that had covered her vocal cords. The doctor told us that it was a very serious vocal cord injury, equivalent to an athlete tearing an ACL. She was immediately placed on vocal rest. Since then, God has healed her and fully restored her voice, and today she's a worship leader at one of the largest churches in the country. She sings in front of thousands of people every week!

Becca's problem seemed to come out of nowhere. It's very common: we seldom see our struggles coming. They're unpredictable. James reminded us of this when he wrote "whenever you face trials." The word "face" in Greek is *peripipto,* which means "to fall into unexpectedly." That's what makes a problem a problem.

3. Struggles comes in different shapes and sizes.

We seldom get bored with the struggles we face because there are a wide variety of them. Have you ever tried to match paint shades on your walls to samples in the store? The Greek word for "many kinds" is literally translated "multicolored." Our struggles come in many shades and varieties. They vary in intensity and in duration. Some are minor inconveniences, and some are catastrophic. Some of our struggles were custom made to teach us things we would never have learned any other way.

4. Struggles are purposeful.

There's purpose in our pain. Struggles can teach us a lot. As C. S. Lewis puts it: "God whispers to us in our pleasures . . . but shouts in our pain."[1] James 1:2–4 explains that there are three purposes for the struggles we face:

- They purify us.

James 1:3 uses the word "testing," as in testing gold and silver. A goldsmith heats gold and silver until all the impurities burn off. Job 23:10 says, "And when he tests me, I will come out as pure as gold" (NLT). Trials test our faith and purify us. Faith develops when things don't go as we planned and when we don't feel like doing what we know is right. Struggles can make us like steel—when we're tested, we come out stronger. Someone once asked a silversmith, "How do you know when the silver is pure?" He responded, "When I can see my reflection in it." How do we know when we've learned the lessons God is teaching us through our struggles? When God can see His reflection in us, He knows we've been refined.

- They give us endurance.

James 1:3 says the testing of our faith "produces perseverance." Here, the author was talking about staying power and endurance—the ability to keep on keeping on, the ability to hang in there. The Greek means "the ability to stay under pressure." We don't like pressure, and we do everything we can to avoid it. In fact, most people attempt to escape from it through sleeping pills, drugs, alcohol, entertainment, food, etc. But God uses problems and struggles in our lives to teach us how to handle pressure so we never give up.

How does God teach us patience? He even teaches us patience in bumper-to-bumper traffic, in grocery lines, when we're with annoying people, and when we have to wait.

- They help us grow.

Struggles can make us stronger because they help us grow and mature. James wrote, "The testing of your faith produces perseverance . . . so that you may be mature and complete, not lacking anything" (vv. 3–4). That's God's long-range goal for your life, marriage, and family relationships. The ultimate purpose is maturity—that we would gradually become more like Jesus.

God has a way of turning all our struggles around for our good if we let Him. One of the most quoted passages in the Bible is Romans 8:28: "We know that in all things God works for the good of those who love him, who have been called according to his purpose." Though not all things *are* good, this scripture promises that God will make all things work together *for* good.

God is much more interested in building our character than He is in making us comfortable.
—RODNEY AND MICHELLE GAGE

When you read the instructions on how to make chocolate cake, you first learn what ingredients you need: eggs, milk, butter, unsweetened cocoa, baking soda, baking powder, vanilla, etc. However, if you eat raw eggs by themselves, they're horrible. No one eats a stick of butter by itself (well, some might), no one eats baking soda by itself, and . . . you get the point! But when you mix it all together, put it in the oven, and let it bake, you get a delicious chocolate cake. That's what God wants to do with the struggles we experience. He can take something bitter and make it better. His plan is *greater* than what you are going through. The next time you and your spouse go through struggles or one of your children faces hardships in school or relationally, remember to turn the *i* into *e*—this shift allows our struggles to make us *better* rather than *bitter*.

TAKEAWAYS

God never wastes a hurt. There's purpose even in our pain. The opening story in this chapter concerning our son Luke allowed him to learn an incredible lesson. If he hadn't gone through being in a wheelchair for nearly three years, he may have never learned what his greatest strength was. It was while he was in a wheelchair that he discovered his passion for music. During that time when he wasn't very mobile, he learned to play the guitar and keyboard. Today, he's a worship leader, singer, songwriter, photographer, video editor, whiz with technology, and a freakishly talented musician. He found his greatest strengths through one of his greatest struggles. Only God can take our setbacks and turn them into comebacks if we will let Him.

Success is to be measured not so much
by the position that one has reached in life
as by the obstacles which he has overcome.
—BOOKER T. WASHINGTON

Of course, it's no fun to go through struggles, but God allows us to go through them so that we will ultimately depend upon him and grow in every area of our lives. It's through our weaknesses that God can show His strength and power. Peter reminds us:

> Dear friends, don't be surprised at the fiery trials you are going through, as if something strange were happening to you. Instead, be very glad—for these trials make you partners with Christ in his suffering, so that you will have the wonderful joy of seeing his glory when it is revealed to all the world. . . . So if you are suffering in a manner that pleases God, keep on doing what is right, and trust your lives to the God who created you, for he will never fail you. (1 Peter 4:12–13, 19 NLT)

Through our struggles, we craft a story that God will use to comfort and inspire others. It's a law of life: Only those who have walked in our shoes have the credibility to speak words of truth and life to us, and only when we've learned to trust God through our struggles will we be able to impart courage to the people around us, particularly those who watch us most closely—our spouses and children.

We want to leave you with two crucial takeaways:

Find the greater purpose
Instead of asking "Why?" ask "What now?"

- What is God teaching me through my painful circumstances?
- How can I grow from them?
- How can I allow the struggles in my marriage to bring greater patience and understanding in my relationship with my spouse?

- How can I teach my children to grow stronger through their struggles?
- What hidden strengths is God showing me through these times of difficulty?
- How can we profit from our problems as a family?

If we look hard enough, we can always find a greater purpose for our pain and problems. God has a way of directing us, inspecting us, and perfecting us. We (Rodney and Michelle) have learned that many couples and families have difficulty seeing the good in all the bad. It's easy to get overwhelmed with the bad, but in these times, God often reveals our greatest purposes.

Is God trying to direct you? Maybe God is allowing the struggles in your life right now to get your attention. Maybe you're standing at the fork of the road right now and you're trying to make some important decisions concerning your future. Maybe God wants you to take some time to inspect what's going on in your situation. Are you overlooking something important? What is God preparing you for? Having been married for over twenty-eight years, we've learned that God uses us in each season of our lives, but before we enter the next season, God wants to prepare us by perfecting us.

In his book *Necessary Endings*, Dr. Henry Cloud talks about how the good can't begin until the bad ends. Life is about endings and new beginnings. Life has seasons, stages, and phases. This is what growth is about. If there is no growth, we become stagnant. Getting to the next level *always* means leaving something behind and moving forward. Some endings are natural and some are forced. Cloud uses the illustration of a rose bush to teach us that we have to prune toxic, dead, or unwanted things. A rose bush only has enough resources to feed so many buds to their full potential. It can't bring all of them into full bloom. In order for the bush to thrive, a certain number of buds have to go. Some of the buds are good but not the best, sick but not getting well, and there are ones that have long been dead. The caretaker carefully and regularly examines those that need to be pruned and makes the cuts.[2]

If we accept the premise that we'll need to prune but have a great deal of emotional discomfort about it, we'll struggle to realize our potential. We need to understand that endings are normal and change our mind-set so we accept and even welcome them. If we see our struggles as normal and expected, we can let God use them to direct us, inspect us, and perfect us.

Find a way to help others through their struggles

It's easy to sit around in self-pity or blame others for the problems we face, but at some point, we have to take the focus off ourselves and place it on others. God allows pain so we can learn from our struggles. In fact, overcoming our struggles is a big part of our story. It doesn't take long to discover someone else who's dealing with bigger problems than ours. The legendary basketball coach John Wooden once said, "You can't live a perfect day without doing something for someone who will never be able to repay you."[3]

Who better to encourage someone who has been diagnosed with cancer than someone who has had cancer? Who better to encourage someone who has experienced the pain of divorce than someone who has gone through it themselves? Who better to give hope and help to someone going through financial difficulties than someone who has lost everything? You get the point. There are always people who are waiting to be helped with the comfort and care that only those who've experience their struggle can give. In the words of Sally Koch, "Great opportunities to help others seldom come, but small ones surround us daily."[4]

Remember, every family ends up somewhere, but few families

end up somewhere on purpose. Follow your GPS—your goals, passions, and the lessons you've learned from your struggles. No matter where you've come from and what hurdles you still need to jump over, you can make the shift. You can trust God to be there every step of the way!

 THINK ABOUT IT:

1. Do you agree or disagree with the statement that our struggles can make us bitter or better? Explain your answer.

2. Struggles are inevitable, are unpredictable, come in many shapes and sizes, and are purposeful. What did you learn about struggles from this chapter? What kind of struggles are you facing right now?

3. Which of the three ways mentioned in James 1:2–4 has God used struggles in your life?

4. Could God be using your current circumstances and struggles to direct you, inspect you, or perfect you? Which one of these do you think He is using right now in your life, marriage, or family relationships?

5. What is the story God wants to tell through your struggles? What's holding you back from sharing that story? Who do you know right now that God wants you to encourage? Or, if you're currently facing a struggle, how might you use this struggle as part of a story to tell others when you've overcome it?

6. What areas of growth do you need to help your kids with? Taking their goals, passions, and struggles into consideration, is there a hidden strength that God wants to use for His greater purpose?

7. What did you learn from the illustration of the rose bush? What needs to be pruned in your life?

 DO IT:

1. Think of one person who's struggling right now (it may be the person sleeping next to you or down the hall). With grace and empathy, step into that person's life to show you care. Talk little and listen much.

STEP 4

FIND LIFE-GIVING FRIENDSHIPS

A SHIFT IN REINFORCEMENT

CHAPTER 10

IRON SHARPENS IRON

Teach Your Kids the Difference between Companions and Confidants

---

When you place your trust in another person,
you'll get one of two results:
A friend for life, or a lesson for life. Both are valuable.

—RODNEY AND MICHELLE GAGE

Have you ever used jumper cables before? If you haven't, you've likely seen someone else use them to help jump-start another vehicle with a dead battery. Recently, my (Rodney's) car wouldn't start, so I asked a friend to pull his vehicle up next to mine so the jumper cables would reach both our cars. My friend opened up the hood and told me to go ahead and latch the cables onto the battery of my car. After I put the red (positive) and the black (negative) cables onto my car's correct battery terminals my friend proceeded to put his end of the cables onto his battery terminals. However, I noticed he was getting ready to clamp the (black) negative cable onto the (red) positive terminal.

Quickly, I shouted, "Wait! Don't put the negative onto the positive!"

My terrified friend asked, "Why? What difference will it make?"

I said, "If you have the negative on the positive and start your engine, it can damage the engine and potentially cause the battery to burst!"

When you think about it, the same is true with friendships. Our friends are either a plus or a minus. Negative influence can cause serious problems in our lives if we're not careful. Nothing can cause us to drift faster and further away from our mission and vision for our marriage and family than negative influences.

If we get our friendships right, our friends can help set us up for success in every area of our lives. The opposite is also true: If we get our friendships wrong, the wrong friends can set us up for a whole lot of pain, regret, disappointment, or even destruction. As the old saying goes, "Show me your friends and I will show you your future." As we move into the fourth step of our 5-Step Plan to stop the drift and start living with greater intention, there is another shift we need to make. It's what we call the shift in reinforcement. Without a clear vision for our future, strong moral values we hold in our hearts, and an understanding of how to use our GPS, we are vulnerable to what my pastor friend Ed Young calls the "sway of they."[1]

If we're insecure about who we are and what we believe on the inside, our temptation and vulnerability is to cave in to the pressures from the outside. The norm is to conform on the path of popularity. This is what most parents fear the most—a child or teenager conforming to the negative influences of their peers and popular culture. That's why the apostle Paul warned, "Do not be misled: 'Bad company corrupts good character'" (1 Corinthians 15:33).

As parents, one of the most important gifts we can give our kids is the wisdom to pick good friends. We make a huge mistake when we assume "they'll find good friends." Yes, they may, but it's our responsibility to steer them toward life-giving friendships. But before we focus on them, let's talk about you and me.

One of the greatest impacts we can have on our kids is to show them the power of choosing the right kind of friendships. What kind of friends do you currently associate with? What kind of values do they have? What kind of influence do they have on your marriage, family, and the choices you make? According to business icon and entrepreneur Jim Rohn, "you are the average of the five people you spend the most time with."[2] If that statement is true, on a scale of one to ten, how would you rate yourself with the five people you and your spouse spend the most time with? How are they influencing you on a professional, spiritual, financial, parental, and relational level? Here is a motto we have found to be very true that can affect us in a positive way or a negative way:

Where you go determines who you meet.
Who you meet determines how you think.
How you think determines what you do.
What you do determines who you become.

In chapter 1, we discussed the essential question for this book: Who do you want to become? This is a vital question because our answers determine the kind of friendships and associations we will pursue in life. You may discover that you are one relationship away from shifting your future in the right direction. The same is true for your kids if they learn to choose the right friends.

REFRAMING FRIENDSHIPS

In the blink of an eye, the popular concept of friendship has changed. One study reveals the average American today only has two close friends; in the mid- to late '80s, the average American reported having three. Even more alarming is that nearly half of the adults polled could only list one name.[3] I believe friendships are under stress for three main reasons: (1) longer work hours due to technology enabling us to answer emails and check documents long after leaving the office, (2) rising divorce rates that rupture networks of relationships, and (3) the explosion of social media that has redefined what it means to be a "friend." Many people are obsessed with their online image and neglect face-to-face connections. Social media is no longer a supplement for relationships; it's a replacement. In a message on friendships, Tim Keller says there are four crucial components: constancy, carefulness, candor, and counsel. He summarizes the four: "A true friend always lets you in and never lets you down."[4]

Years ago, we met a young dating couple and really hit it off with them. As we got to know them, we led the young man to Christ, and before long, I (Rodney) performed their wedding. We enjoyed seeing them grow in their relationships with each other and in their relationships with God. Before long, we became very close. They were among our closest friends and confidants.

After a couple of years or so, we sensed some distance in our relationship with them. We wondered what we'd done that might have offended them. We tried to talk to them, but they said, "Oh, there's no problem. Everything is fine." But we knew it wasn't. After a few weeks, we discovered they had been hanging around some other couples and doing things they normally wouldn't do. This other group was very toxic and seemed to take delight in being critical and negative.

We hoped to mend any rifts in the relationship, so we asked our friends to have coffee with us. As we talked, they informed us that they were leaving our church. We felt confused and frustrated. Maybe *betrayed* is a better word to describe our emotions. We had invested our time, hearts, and love in them. We'd walked with them through some serious storms in their lives, and now they were turning their backs on us. As we drove away from our visit with them we were deeply hurt, confused, and, needless to say, disappointed that our friendship with them had come to an end.

Our children saw us walk through this difficult and painful season. We told them enough of what had happened so they understood our shock and heartache. They felt our pain. We talked with them many times about whether we can trust people, and if we can, how much and how fast. Our kids saw us feel the hurt, but they also saw us choose to forgive, refuse to speak negative words about the couple, and learn hard-won lessons about the value and vulnerability of friendships.

Your tribe determines your vibe.
—RODNEY AND MICHELLE GAGE

As parents, we're imprinting images and values on our children from the time they're born. What they see is what they believe is good and right and normal. If they see resentment and estrangement, they'll believe all people are enemies and they should be suspicious toward others. If they see apathy, they'll conclude that relationships aren't really important at all. But if they see genuine, strong, give-and-take friendships, they'll understand that choosing and building good friends is a crucial part of life. The message to them begins with us. The quality of our friendships has a dramatic impact on what our kids value in the people they choose as friends.

As I mentioned earlier, the "sway of they" can be powerful and, at times, detrimental to us and our kids fulfilling our destinies. If we don't hold to strong beliefs and values on the inside, we will cave in to the pressures on the outside.

THE BAD NEWS

We know that girls' bodies typically mature earlier than boys', but by mid-adolescence, the boys have caught up. Before long, both groups look like young adults, and parents usually expect them to act like young adults. But there's a problem: The prefrontal cortexes of their brains continue to develop until they're about twenty-five years old. This is the part of the brain that is responsible for "executive function," reasoning that is essential for making good decisions. Before this part of the brain develops, youths rely more on the amygdala, which is part of "the reptilian brain" and is associated with impulsive decisions, emotions, and instinct. In addition, the limbic system is also active in adolescents before the prefrontal cortex is fully developed. This part of the brain controls risk and reward. This combination of factors means teenagers naturally seek adventure, but they lack the ability to process information that adults interpret as stop signs. They live far more by impulse than they will later.[5]

Neurobiologist Dr. Frances Jensen has studied the adolescent brain and recommends that parents realize adolescent thinking patterns are different:

> They're experiencing emotion in Technicolor, whereas we're experiencing it in black and white. And it makes you understand a bit more why they behave the way they do....
>
> [Teenage love] feels very real to the person in that moment. It's bona fide emotion; it's just not emotion that's measured like it will be later in life, where you might say, "I'm attracted to this person, but there's a lot of reasons why this may not be." It's real but just feels unbridled. Teens have superheated limbic systems, so the emotional areas, the sexual incentive areas, are on.[6]

This is why helping our kids choose the right associations and stay true to their core beliefs and values is so vital to helping them fulfill God's best for their lives.

THREE VITAL FRIENDSHIPS

Your kids need to see you investing in and enjoying three types of friendships: your friendship with God, your friendship with your spouse, and your friendships with a few other close companions. As they watch, they'll realize the value of each of these connections.

With God

It's a stunning fact that God, the infinite, omniscient, all-powerful Creator of the universe, wants the kind of relationship with us that can be called a friendship. Jesus spent an extended time with His closest followers on the night He knew He would be arrested. They had heard Him teach and seen Him do miracles for over three years. Now, when it was time for Him to die, He wanted to leave them with important messages. He told them:

> "I've told you these things for a purpose: that my joy might be your joy, and your joy wholly mature. This is my command: Love one another the way I loved you. This is the very best way to love. Put your life on the line for your friends. You are my friends when you do the things I command you. I'm no longer calling you servants because servants don't understand what their master is thinking and planning. No, I've named you friends because I've let you in on everything I've heard from the Father." (John 15:11–15 MSG)

Do you relate to God as a friend? Many of us don't. Our relationships with God are, to a large extent, formed by our relationships with our parents. If they were harsh, we typically believe God is demanding and condemning. If they were distant, we usually believe God doesn't really care. But if they were fairly consistent in their affection, wisdom, and presence, we are likely to believe God cares, He's present, and we can trust Him.

With your spouse

Marriage can become stale. The rigors of juggling schedules, financial headaches, the constant demands of parenting, pressures from in-laws, and differences in sexual appetites can erode the joy and creativity of the first years of marriage until the two people are little more than roommates—roommates who barely tolerate each other. Studies by Dr. John Gottman, who is world-renowned for his research on marriage stability and divorce prediction, show that, of all the facets of a marriage relationship, the one that is the most significant predictor of a healthy marriage is friendship.[7] Enjoying and trusting each other oils the complex mechanism of competing schedules, desires, and expectations. Bill Hanawalt, executive pastor of Vineyard Christian Church in Evanston, Illinois, observes:

> Marriage without friendship cannot work in our culture. . . . Friendship has to be nourished and nurtured regularly or it faces the danger of becoming a business relationship. I have seen many distant and businesslike marriages where careers have developed and children have come into the picture, and the priority of emotional connection has been left to die on the vine. Couples that don't give attention to developing their friendship often come apart. It also creates an opening for marital infidelity.[8]

To continue to build a strong friendship in marriage, each person needs to invest time, energy, and heart. Little things matter: Pay attention when the other person is talking, stimulate the other person's creativity, do chores together, forgive offenses (real or imagined), and make the relationship a priority rather than taking it for granted.

With others

Solomon gave the clearest, most succinct commentary on the power of relationships: "Walk with the wise and become wise; associate with fools and get in trouble" (Proverbs 13:20 NLT). We see it all the time. When we spend time with people who are pursuing God and His purposes with all their hearts, their passion rubs off on us. And when we spend time with people who value success, pleasure, and approval more than anything, their perspective awakens discontent, comparison, and unhealthy competition.

Some of us are from families that have crippled us emotionally and relationally. We bear the scars of years of harm. For a few, the damage came like hammer blows, but for others, constant criticism wore away our self-confidence like sandpaper on a pine board. We may have had painful relationships with those we counted on in the past, but God can give us a new family, His family. Again, we turn to Solomon, who wrote: "There are 'friends' who destroy each other, but a real friend sticks closer than a brother" (Proverbs 18:24 NLT).

I know a lot of people who can testify to this truth. They felt abandoned or abused in their childhoods, but they've found new brothers and sisters in the spiritual family through their local churches. We believe church can be the perfect place for imperfect people. Of course, not everyone who comes to church can be a true friend. Church is full of broken people, sinful people, people who have suffered from "destroyed" relationships for any number of reasons. But church is also the place where God does deep work in our hearts—healing wounds, imparting wisdom, and building trust. Friends are with us in our darkest times, and they don't laugh, run away, or give us simplistic answers to life's deepest problems.

Choose friends who celebrate you, not tolerate you.
—ED YOUNG

LAYERS OF FRIENDSHIPS

In our lives, and we suspect in yours, it's easy to identify three distinct layers of friendships: surface, structured, and secure. We can know someone for years but never connect beyond a *surface* level. We talk about the weather, or a sports team, or something happening in town, but we don't move past the level of facts. We may have hundreds or even thousands of connections like this.

We have a deeper level of connections with people who have shared interests with us. These are *structured* relationships. We're in a club, we work together, our kids are on the same team, or we play tennis with them. These people have at least some idea of what we value, and they affirm what we believe. They're cheerleaders when we do well, and they overlook most of our faults. We may have dozens of these people in our lives.

In the third layer are those who give us *security*. Beyond facts and shared interests, we have shared hearts with these people. We delight in the same things, and we grieve over the same losses. These are the people who show up at the worst moments of our lives, and these are the people who celebrate our successes instead of feeling threatened by our progress. We don't have many friends like this, and we don't need many—maybe two or three at a time. If we are the average of the five people we spend the most time with, these are the kind of people we should pursue in our friendships.

Today, social media has changed our definition of "friends." We may have thousands of friends on Facebook and a similar number on Instagram, but we carefully craft the "face" we let people see. We do more posing than sharing. There's nothing wrong with these super-ficial connections as long as they're not the only kind we have. If we fail to go to the two deeper levels, we'll assume that the number of likes tells us how many true friends we have, and we'll miss out on authentic, soul-nourishing connections with a few people.

Our circle of friends usually changes as we enter new stages of life or move to new communities. And sometimes, our interests change, so we gain new friends around the new endeavors. In their book, *Relationships*, psychologists Les and Leslie Parrott identify "friends of the road" and "friends of the heart." They explain:

> With most friendships, new concerns and new faces gradu-ally crowd out the old as we start a new journey. But not with committed friends. They don't flicker and fade; they keep the lights on. They are there for the duration and are as elemental to our being as blood to our heart.
>
> Are friendships of the heart more important than our fleeting friends of the road? Not really. We need both. What matters is how a relationship sustains you right now. An achieved friendship—of any brand or bond—is among the best experiences life has to offer.[9]

We may impress people with our strengths,
but we connect with people through our weaknesses.
—CRAIG GROESCHEL

MENDING THE BROKEN PLACES

Some of the most painful times in our lives occur when we experience conflict with people we love and trust. All significant relationships are messy from time to time, so we need to understand how to mend them when they're broken. The cause of the fracture may be any number of things, including unrealistic expectations on the part of one person leading the other to feel smothered, the clash of political perspectives, differences of opinion about raising children, one person moving to another city, busyness that gradually causes the friendship to cool, and the dagger thrust of betrayal.

We probably have no need to mend broken relationships on the superficial level because there's not enough emotional vulnerability to expose us to hurt. On the structured layer, however, shared interests can lead to sharp disagreements. A shared purpose can unite us, but different strategies can divide us. The measure of hurt in relationships is directly proportional to the level of trust. When we're vulnerable, we share what's in our hearts, which can be wonderfully healing or terribly damaging. Let us offer some suggestions for healing the fractures in any significant relationship:

Be honest with yourself

Many people let hurt turn into anger, which then turns into bitterness, all because they don't want to admit they're hurt. Denial never leads to healing and reconciliation. Before we find the courage and the right words to talk to the other person, we need to take time for some self-reflection. If the pain is overwhelming, it's wise to get the comfort and advice of someone who has been down this road before and found hope and healing along the way.

Prepare for the talk

We often make one of two mistakes when we try to resolve a disagreement: we run in too quickly or we hesitate too long. We need a combination of good preparation and plenty of courage. Before talking to the person, carefully think out what you want to say and how you want to say it. Try to see the issue from the other person's point of view so you can empathize. Try to find common ground, and realize the person will almost certainly have a different point of view. You'll have to decide, before the conversation, how much to push back and how much to let go. Don't set the time to talk until you're prepared. (It's usually wise to bounce your plan off someone who is wise and objective.)

Speak up and speak respectfully

When we wade in to talk to someone about a problem in a relationship, some of us use intimidation to get our way, and some just want to get the talk over as soon as possible. If we're prepared, we can say what we planned to say, and then listen to the response. Our goal isn't to force the other person to agree with us (that's manipulation), but to find some common ground so we can make progress in the relationship. It's wise to begin by sharing your painful feelings: "I feel hurt," or "I feel angry," or "I feel afraid." Then describe the problem, try to empathize "You probably see it this way . . .," and say, "I want us to have a healthier relationship. Here are some steps we can take." Or you might say, "Here are some steps *I'm* going to take."

Don't expect instant resolution

Sometimes when we bring up hard things to others, they respond very well and immediately—but that's very rare. Far more often, they're defensive or evasive. Expect this kind of response, and give the person time to think about it before you talk again in a day or two.

Forgive

Forgiveness is unilateral, but reconciliation takes both. We can forgive the person who hurt us whether that person ever admits the wrong or changes. We forgive because Jesus has forgiven us (Ephesians 4:32), but we're foolish to trust someone who hasn't proven to be trustworthy. Reconciliation usually takes time, and it can't happen until and unless the other person admits the wrong, genuinely grieves the pain caused, and makes a commitment (and follows through) to never do it again.

It is by forgiving that one is forgiven.
—MOTHER TERESA

Rebuild trust

Some fractures in relationships are minor and can be repaired fairly easily. In fact, when they're over, we wonder why we didn't resolve things sooner! But others involve severe breaches of trust and years of lies and wounds. In these cases, both sides have to put in plenty of time and hard work to rebuild the relationship. The good news is that if both people are willing, God can do amazing things.

A woman came to talk to me (Rodney) after her divorce. I listened as she told me about how her ex-husband had put his time and heart in his career instead of spending time with her or their children. She was heartbroken. I asked if her ex would come with her next time. He agreed, and again she told her story about his lack of interest in her and the children. To my surprise, he wasn't defensive and he didn't blame her. He nodded to affirm that all she was saying was true. His honesty was a huge open door for reconciliation!

I met with him several times. He trusted in Christ and started attending our church. In time, his agenda, his life's mission, vision, and values were radically transformed. During all this, I gave him some specific things to do to rekindle the relationship. He took his former wife on dates, and he made the reservations; he called her during the day to tell her he loved her; and they soon invited their kids to go to dinner and other activities with them. Her heartache was healed by his authentic and consistent displays of love. Months later, he called to ask me to perform their second marriage. It was a wonderful restoration of what selfishness had broken. She finally felt cherished and safe, and the kids had a loving, attentive father for the first time in their lives. All this started because she came to me with a broken heart.

Depending on the nature of the relationship, we don't necessarily have to reconstruct the same level of trust and vulnerability as we had before the strain. We need to weigh the benefits and count the costs. Some connections are so valuable that we'll do anything to repair them, but many, especially in the structured category, aren't high enough on our priority list to take time away from our most important relationships to do the time-consuming work of rebuilding. Even then, it's our responsibility to forgive, to speak kindly of the person, and to drift gently apart with no animosity.

When the right people come into your life,
you'll understand why the wrong ones had to leave.
—RODNEY GAGE

What does all this have to do with families? Everything! If our children see us avoiding hard conversations, they'll believe they aren't competent to resolve the struggles they have with people. Then, the two options are fight or flight—demanding and intimidating others or hiding physically or emotionally. But if they see us enjoying our most important relationships and doing the hard work to keep them strong, they'll learn valuable lessons about the importance of great friendships . . . and they'll make a crucial shift toward becoming wise adults.

THINK ABOUT IT:

1. How would you paraphrase this statement: "True friends always let you in and never let you down"?
2. What is your level of fear about your children developing healthy friendships? Why?
3. What is your relationship like with God, with your spouse, and with a few of your best friends? Are any improvements needed in any of those areas?
4. How would you evaluate the quality and quantity of your three layers of friends: surface, structured, and secure?
5. As you've observed friendships over the years, what factors have caused the most strains and fractures?
6. How confident are you in taking steps to try to reconcile relationships that have been broken?
7. Why is it important to differentiate forgiveness from trust and reconciliation?
8. What do your children see when they watch you and your friends?

 DO IT:

1. Have a conversation with your spouse and talk about your most encouraging and your most painful friendships.
2. Have a conversation with your kids and tell them about your best friends and those that weren't so positive. (Let your descriptions be age appropriate.)

CHAPTER 11

EVERY FRIENDSHIP NEEDS A LITTLE TLC

Consider Character When Choosing Friends

Show me who you're listening to
and I will show you who you are becoming.

—RODNEY AND MICHELLE GAGE

Not too long ago, as I (Rodney) was grilling on our back porch, I heard a very unusual sound. I opened the screen door and saw an owl in a big bush outside. I ran inside and grabbed Michelle and the kids. I didn't want to scare the bird, so I whispered as loud as I could, "Y'all come out to see this . . . and be real quiet!"

When they joined me on the porch, I pointed to the owl in the bush, but none of them saw it. It was right there in front of them, but they couldn't see it. I pointed and described it until Michelle and the kids could see the big, beautiful bird. It had been in plain sight all along! We stood in silence and amazement. There's no telling how long this wonderful creature had been sitting quietly in the bush next to our door. We could have enjoyed it sooner if we had known where to look.

Owls are interesting creatures. In our part of the country, and especially in our neighborhood, they're rare, and they're difficult to see because they blend into their natural habitat. Usually, someone else has to point them out and say, "Look—there it is!" But when owls hoot, it's unmistakable. Their sound is a sure sign one of them is nearby.

Wise people are like this owl. They usually blend in with the crowd. They may be still and quiet for a long time as they observe what is going on around them, but when they speak up, everyone else knows they've heard the sound of true wisdom. Solomon, one of the wisest men who ever lived, was right when he said in Proverbs 13:20, "Walk with the wise and become wise, for a companion of fools suffers harm."

One of the wisest things we can do from time to time is to take what we call a "friendatory." Ask yourself the question, *How is my friending trending?* As we learned in the previous chapter, our friends are either a plus or a minus. They are either inspiring us to reach our full potential or causing us to drift. If we want to avoid drifting away from the things that matter most in our lives, we need to surround ourselves with wise people. Like the owl, wise people are not always easy to recognize at first. They tend not to draw a lot of attention to themselves. We have learned from our own experiences with friendships that a few characteristics stand out among wise friends. We call these the TLC of friendship. Wise friends are tough, loyal, and committed.

TOUGH

In the summer before I (Rodney) entered the seventh grade, our family moved from Houston to Dallas. My parents knew I wanted to find some new friends, so they introduced me to the son of a couple they knew. Beasley and I became great friends, and he helped me make the transition to a new city, a new school, and a lot of new kids. He was highly respected for his athletic skills and his strong commitment to Christ. As school started, he took me under his wing and made me feel accepted. He set me up for success in relationships, which, as you undoubtedly know, is quite a challenge for a new kid in junior high school.

One day in the locker room, the older boys were harassing the younger kids like me. They used their size and numbers to intimidate us, hoisting smaller students up to hang by their belt loops on hooks on the wall. When they came at me, my friend Beasley walked in, saw what was happening, and stood between the other boys and me. He told them, "If you want to get him, you'll have to go through me! You're not going to treat my friend that way!" He could have turned around and walked out without saying a word, or he could have joined them in intimidating me, but he stood up for me at the risk of his reputation and safety. I had a friend I could count on. Beasley eventually became my college roommate and the best man in my wedding.

We sometimes use the word "tough" as a negative to say someone is mean. That's not our definition here. We're talking about people who have strong convictions and are not affected by the "sway of they" and other people's opinions. Some people are like chameleons: they change their moods, words, and actions to please the person in front of them. Others are critical and sarcastic, attempting to cover up their insecurities by putting others down. And some people are so needy they're like leeches that suck the life out of everyone they know. They sound pitiful to convince people to help them, take care of them, and give them what they want. The people who help may feel compassion at first . . . until they realize they're being played. But we (Rodney and Michelle) have had the pleasure of being friends with people who exhibit quiet confidence.

These people know who they are, and they're secure. In their relationships, they can give as well as take. They have developed (and are continuing to develop) convictions about what's most important to them. But they realize everything isn't a big deal, so they can let some things slide. Only a few things are hills worth dying on, and they're willing to go there because they're convinced those things are of ultimate importance.

People who model this kind of toughness stand their ground in hard times. They have a vision for their lives and stand firm in their values and beliefs. Throughout history, few have exemplified this characteristic of spiritual and relational toughness more than the prophet Daniel and his three friends, Shadrach, Meshach, and Abednego. After the Babylonians conquered God's people and sent the best and brightest young Israelite men into exile to serve the king, the Babylonian court made demands on them. Daniel and his three friends were in this group.

Part of the training was to give the young men a particular diet—one that didn't conform to Jewish dietary law. If they ate it, they would dishonor God, but if they didn't eat it, they might be killed. Before we go any further, think about their predicament: Their homeland had been devastated. It appeared that God had abandoned them to a cruel fate, and they were hundreds of miles from home, with no prospect of ever getting back. Their captors were demanding compliance, and the Israelites had already seen how the Babylonians dealt with resistance! It would have been very easy to buckle under the disappointment and pressure, but Daniel didn't do that. "Daniel purposed in his heart that he would not defile himself with the portion of the king's delicacies, nor with the wine which he drank; therefore he requested of the chief of the eunuchs that he might not defile himself" (Daniel 1:8 NKJV).

Daniel won the admiration of the chief steward with his character, so Daniel had an open door to make him an offer. He and his friends would eat only vegetables and drink water for ten days. After that, if they appeared strong and healthy, the steward wouldn't demand they eat the training meals. "And at the end of ten days their features appeared better and fatter in flesh than all the young men who ate the portion of the king's delicacies. Thus the steward took away their portion of delicacies and the wine that they were to drink, and gave them vegetables" (Daniel 1:15–16 NKJV). These four friends took a big risk to trust God to make them strong off of vegetables while others enjoyed steaks. It took courage. It took conviction. They were as tough as nails spiritually and morally.

The rest of the story reveals that their conviction about food gave them courage to face any obstacle and demand. In Daniel 3, we see how three of them (Shadrach, Meshach, and Abednego) trusted God in the face of seemingly certain death when the king threw them into a fiery furnace because of their refusal to bow down and worship a golden image. Do you think they would have had the strength to be strong in that moment if they hadn't trusted God together earlier about the food and drink? Courage stimulates courage in those around us, and spiritual and moral toughness is an example for others to follow.

But toughness doesn't always come out in fierce determination. We also need friends who encourage us to be strong enough to be tender. The apostle Paul was one of the toughest leaders the world has ever known. He suffered ridicule and beatings, shipwrecks and stoning, homelessness and hunger. All of this could have made him cynical, but instead, he appreciated God's love more than ever. If we're strong in grace, we'll be kind to others—especially those who are hard to love. Paul explained it this way:

Since God chose you to be the holy people he loves, you must clothe yourselves with tenderhearted mercy, kindness, humility, gentleness, and patience. Make allowance for each other's faults, and forgive anyone who offends you. Remember, the Lord forgave you, so you must forgive others. Above all, clothe yourselves with love, which binds us all together in perfect harmony. (Colossians 3:12–14 NLT)

We can't love the unlovely and show God's kindness to those who want to hurt us unless we possess incredible inner strength . . . unless we're tough like Paul and Daniel and his friends.

Are we the kind of friends who have strong convictions and an unshakable security in the love of God? If we are, we'll attract people who either have that same strength or are in the process of developing it. These are the kinds of friendships that give us incredible ballast when the seas are rough, and these are the kinds of friendships that launch us to make a difference in the world. Remember we attract who we are.

When someone speaks truth into your life,
you either get mad or you get mature.

—LISA YOUNG

LOYAL

We have a friend who has a daughter named Gabby. When she was a freshman in high school, she had an anchor of a lifelong best friend. We'll call her Suzanne. The two had known each other for years and seemed to be joined at the hip. Both of the girls tried out for the cheerleading team, and both made the cut. But soon after school started, Suzanne became friends with another girl, Marcia. Gabby was happy to have another good friend, but that's not how Suzanne saw things. She became emotionally attached to Marcia, and together, they formed a secret alliance against Gabby. Relational triangles are usually awkward and painful, and this one was no exception. At one point, Gabby realized the other two girls were lying to her and about her. She was deeply hurt. She realized that loyalty kept is beautiful, but loyalty betrayed is devastating.

Life has a way of pulling people apart, causing little annoyances that turn into major disruptions in our most important relationships. But true friends fight through the misunderstandings and competing goals at all costs. Friends are loyal.

The story of David and Jonathan is one of the most beautiful in the Scriptures. Jonathan was King Saul's son, the presumptive heir to the throne. Jonathan and David's relationship began after David's stunning defeat of the giant Goliath. Saul's army was terrified of Goliath, and for weeks they cowered behind their lines as they heard his taunts. David's father asked him to take bread and cheese to his brothers in the army, and when he arrived, he heard Goliath laugh at God's pitiful army. If nobody else would take on the giant, he would! He marched down into the valley armed with only a sling and some rocks. His aim was true, and the giant fell down dead.

When David went to the king to give his report, Jonathan was there. Undoubtedly, he had been one of the amazed soldiers in the audience that day in the valley, and now he saw David, the shepherd boy, up close. First Samuel 18:1–4 tells us:

> By the time David had finished reporting to Saul, Jonathan was deeply impressed with David—an immediate bond was forged between them. He became totally committed to David. From that point on he would be David's number-one advocate and friend.

Saul received David into his own household that day, no more to return to the home of his father.

Jonathan, out of his deep love for David, made a covenant with him. He formalized it with solemn gifts: his own royal robe and weapons—armor, sword, bow, and belt. (MSG)

The tables turned quickly in David's relationship with Saul. The king was jealous—and furious—when he heard people singing, dancing, and giving credit to David for the defeat of the Philistines at his expense. He was so insulted that the next day he tried to kill David with a spear . . . twice! Saul made life miserable for the hero of the nation. He lied to David, cheated him out of a wife, and tried to capture him and kill him. This, of course, put Jonathan in quite a bind. David had every reason to assume his friend would choose his father's side, and he gave him an opportunity to bow out of the friendship. But Jonathan was loyal to David. In fact, Jonathan became a spy for David. He found out his father's plans to capture David and shared the information. When David fled, Saul asked Jonathan why David wasn't eating dinner with them. Jonathan stretched the truth in his reply, and his loyalty to David proved costly.

Saul exploded in anger at Jonathan: "You son of a slut! Don't you think I know that you're in cahoots with the son of Jesse, disgracing both you and your mother? For as long as the son of Jesse is walking around free on this earth, your future in this kingdom is at risk. Now go get him. Bring him here. From this moment, he's as good as dead!" (1 Samuel 20:30–31 MSG)

Jonathan refused to give David up to his father. Later, in a great battle, the Philistines killed both Saul and Jonathan. David became king. It was customary for a king from a new line to kill all the descendants of the prior royalty, but David found Jonathan's son Mephibosheth, who was crippled, and showed extraordinary kindness by bringing him to live in the palace and eat at David's table every day (2 Samuel 9).

For David and Jonathan loyalty worked both ways. Loyalty is measured in the cost of remaining true to someone even when it's inconvenient, when others disagree, and when we lose something valuable. Jonathan was loyal to David at great expense, and David poured kindness on Jonathan's son to fulfill his covenant of love with his friend.

Loyalty says, "No matter what, you can count on me." A true friend celebrates our successes and grieves our losses. That's rare. It's much more common for people we know to be jealous about our successes and to do what they can to cut us down to size. Though they begrudgingly acknowledge our losses, they never enter into our pain.

Conflict always reveals character.
How you respond shows who you really are!
—RODNEY AND MICHELLE GAGE

COMMITTED

Loyalty is the inclination of the heart; commitment leads to actions that reflect this loyalty. True friends show their commitment in acceptance and alignment.

When we accept one another, we have a wonderful blend of grace and truth. We don't just roll over when we see our friend making a dumb decision or having a bad attitude. We love enough to step in and say what needs to be said. This means we say it in the way the friend can hear it, not to "get it off our chests" but to "put it in their hearts." We speak with grace because we've experienced grace. How did Jesus accept the disciples? By inviting them to join Him, overlooking most of their failures and flaws, gently correcting them when necessary, and spending plenty of time with them so they'd experience the full measure of His love for them. That's how Jesus relates to us, too . . . and it's the mark of commitment in friendships.

Two people who have nothing in common rarely form a deep friendship. We need at least some level of alignment of purpose with someone else if we're going to be friends. We need to share similar convictions about what's important and what's trivial, what God wants to do in and through us, and which hill we're willing to die on. In fact, the close bonds soldiers experience in combat are formed by exactly this kind of alignment—they're literally willing to die on the same hill for each other.

The story of Ruth is a beautiful tale of loyalty and alignment. Ruth was a Moabite woman who was considered an outcast by the Jews even though she had married one. They did not accept or embrace those outside of their own race. After both their husbands died, leaving them destitute, Ruth and her mother-in-law, Naomi, decided to walk back to Palestine. As they approached the city of Bethlehem, Naomi had second thoughts. She told Ruth to go back home where she'd feel more comfortable among her own people, but Ruth had other ideas.

> Ruth replied, "Don't ask me to leave you and turn back. Wherever you go, I will go; wherever you live, I will live. Your people will be my people, and your God will be my God. Wherever you die, I will die, and there I will be buried. May the Lord punish me severely if I allow anything but death to separate us!" (Ruth 1:16–17 NLT)

In Naomi's hour of despair, Ruth proved to be much more than a daughter-in-law—she was a committed friend who aligned the direction and future of her life with Naomi's. How strong was her commitment? As strong as death.

The difference between ordinary and extraordinary is that little extra.

—JIMMY JOHNSON

If you're going to make the shift in your personal life and marriage, and if your kids are going to thrive in today's culture, you need to learn to walk with the wise. Doing so is critical to achieving your destiny as a family. Finding friends who are tough will make you bolder and better. Friends who are loyal will be confidants to you and will celebrate you. Friends who are committed will accept you unconditionally and will be in alignment with your mission, vision, and values. They will affirm your goals and passions and walk through your struggles with you.

You might be asking, "How in the world do I find those kinds of people? And do those type of kids exist in elementary, middle, and high school for my children?" The answer is yes! However, we must be that kind of friend in order to have those kinds of friends. Again, you attract who you are. A great exercise for you to work through for yourself, as a couple, and with your kids is to identify the personality traits, characteristics, and qualities you would want to have in a friend. Be very specific. Once you identify those characteristics and qualities, ask yourself, *Am I that kind of person?* As we help our kids think about their friendships and their future mates, it's important to teach and reinforce to them that in order to have the right kinds of friends, we must first be the right kind of friend. Marriage is not about finding the right mate, it's about being the right mate. Before we move on to the fifth and final step of our 5-Step Plan of living with greater intention as a family, let's commit to making the necessary shifts in our current friendships and ask God to bring wise friends into our lives—friends who are tough, loyal, and committed who will help us live with greater intention.

 THINK ABOUT IT:

1. How does this chapter define the quality of being a friend who is tough?
2. Why is tenderness also related to toughness?
3. How have you shown loyalty when a friend was going through a hard time? How did your loyalty affect your friend? How did the experience affect you?
4. Why is the courage to speak the truth in a winsome way an important part of accepting someone?
5. At this point in your life, who are a few people whose purpose and drive are closely aligned with yours? What are some ways you inspire and encourage each other?

 DO IT:

1. In relaxed times with your children, consider asking them questions about their friends. Make these questions appropriate for their age. Don't rush through this. One good question can launch wonderful conversations.
2. Tell your children about your friends when you were their age. Be honest, but appropriate.

3. Answer and discuss these questions as a family:
   - Who would you say are my best friends? What do you see in our relationships?
   - Who are the people in your school (or youth group) who make you feel good about yourself? Tell me about that.
   - Who are the people in your class that you admire? What do you appreciate about them?
   - How does it affect you when people lie to you?
   - Who has been your best friend so far? What makes this person special to you?
   - Who are some people you don't trust? What's that about? (Be careful to avoid sharing names or too much information.)
   - Do you want my feedback about what I see in your friends? (If not, I may still give it when I think it's necessary!)

STEP 5

TEACH
BY EXAMPLE

A SHIFT IN PURPOSE

CHAPTER 12

WHO'S ON POINT?

Lead Intentionally

A leader is one who knows the way,
goes the way, and shows the way.

—JOHN C. MAXWELL

Tom Brady is generally considered the GOAT at the quarterback position—the greatest of all time. It didn't start that way. He started as quarterback for only two seasons at the University of Michigan. He wanted to play in the NFL, but he wasn't drafted until the sixth round in 2000. He was the 199th pick—a place from which very few players, much less quarterbacks, rise to become stars in the league. Brady proved to have all the skills, but even more, the mental tenacity to win. As of this writing, he has led the New England Patriots to nine Super Bowls and they have won six of them.

One of the team's Super Bowl losses came in 2018 when the Philadelphia Eagles beat them by a score of 41 to 33. That year, Brady had set a new record for the most passing yards in the postseason.

With two minutes to play in the game, the Eagles had a five-point lead, and history suggested that Brady would pull out another stunning last-minute victory. But when he dropped back to pass, he was sacked and fumbled. The Eagles recovered, kicked a field goal to push the lead to eight points, and won the game.

When Brady got home, his children were taking the loss as hard as any Patriots fan. Brady recalls, "Benny was crying, Vivi was crying, and they were sad for me and sad for the Patriots." He saw this as a valuable moment in his children's lives: "I just said to them, 'Look, this is a great lesson. We don't always win. We try our best and sometimes it doesn't go the way we want."[1]

Maybe you can relate to that statement. Perhaps your life, your hopes, and your dreams haven't turned out the way you thought they would. The pain of divorce, setbacks with your health, work, or finances may have left you feeling downtrodden. Perhaps your kids haven't made the best choices along the way. Before we go any further, let us just remind you that you have already succeeded by making a commitment to read this book. Sadly, most people just keep drifting further and further away from what could be and should be. They refuse to make the necessary shifts in their lives because they're convinced it's too late. There is too much regret and remorse from past failures. They're convinced that this is the hand they've been dealt and they have to just learn to live with the cards they have left. We don't believe that! We believe you can make a shift in your life, your family, and your goals that will allow you to live with greater intention and purpose. That is why we started this book with a vital and foundational first step—choosing to make a shift in direction.

We can't change the direction of the wind, but we can adjust our sails to always reach our destination. No matter where we are or what season of life we're in we can always start with the end in mind. In step 2, we learned the importance of making a shift in our focus— of defining or redefining what is important to us and the values that guide and protect us. In step 3, we discussed a shift in motivation. Our goals, passions, and struggles are the very things God uses to shape the power of our "why." When we tap into the power of our "why," we are motivated to live with greater intention. In step 4 we learned the importance of making a shift in our reinforcements, because having the right friends will propel us, and the wrong friends will derail us. Our friendships will make or break us when it comes to reaching our destiny. Now, it's time to accomplish the last step in our journey together. Step 5 is all about making a shift in our purpose. How do we do that as parents? We teach by example.

Failure doesn't have to be the end of a dream. It may make us more determined and smart and give us a clearer understanding of what it takes to succeed. However, like we learned in the story of Tom Brady, failure is never final. In a Business Insider article about Brady's example to his kids, writer Abby Jackson points to *Shark Tank* investor Barbara Corcoran, who says she likes to invest in people from economically disadvantaged backgrounds. Corcoran asserts, "My bias toward the poor person coming up is they're usually hungrier. They're more injured. They have more to prove. . . . So they've had a few bumpy endings and they're used to failure, and, my God, what's more important in building a business than failing?"[2]

Tom Brady would likely agree. Losing stinks, but if we learn the lessons it can teach, it becomes the aroma of fertile soil for growth. This perspective is one of the most important ones we can pass to our children.

Remember this: *Your children will become who you are, so be who you want them to be.* This means we lead our families intentionally—not passively, just hoping things will turn out well, but with an eye on the prize of growth in their character. This commitment requires us to shift and keep shifting to continually reinforce the mission, vision, and values we want to instill in our children.

Your kids are watching you . . . like a hawk! Speaking of birds, one of the best analogies for understanding the impact of being a role model for our children is the way ornithologists (bird experts) work with whooping crane chicks. The species has been endangered for many years, so to protect the eggs from raccoons and other animals, experts take the eggs to a secluded place where they incubate and hatch. The first moments and days of the chick's life are crucial. They fixate, or "imprint," on whatever is around them. In the wild, it would be their mothers and fathers. In the pen, the ornithologists dress up in whooping crane outfits, using their extended arm and hand as the neck and head of the gigantic bird. The chicks connect with the "parents," and in a few weeks, they have an easy and smooth transition to the established flock because real whooping cranes look like the parents in the pen![3]

This principle doesn't just work with birds; we see it in relationships between parents and children too. Most experts state that young animals, like chicks or our children, get their security and identity by watching parents and emulating them. Our children absorb our attitudes and values almost effortlessly—for them anyway. As they watch, imprinting happens naturally, normally, and necessarily. It happens *naturally* because that's the way God made the parent-child relationship; it happens *normally* in the everyday events of life; and it happens *necessarily* because our kids desperately need good values to become healthy, productive adults. The flip side, of course, is that passive parents don't do enough to instill these values, and harsh parents instill counterproductive values that have an impact on children for the rest of their lives.

Of course, this doesn't mean that we automatically become exactly like our parents. Some of us become carbon copies of one or both of them, but many of us react and become the opposite. For instance, one might expect a harsh, condemning father to have a son who is just like him, but it's very likely he may produce a son who is gentle, compliant, and lives to please the people around him. Both the angry person and the kind person feel equally insecure, but they try to protect themselves and find meaning in very different ways.

All of us imprinted on our parents, and our kids are imprinting on us. The good news is that the values and behaviors we pick up as children can be changed.

> We can't become who we need to be
> by remaining who we are.
>
> —RODNEY AND MICHELLE GAGE

GOD AS OUR MODEL

Jesus didn't just show up at a few events to teach and heal the sick. He spent over three years, day and night, with His closest followers. They saw Him interact with the religious leaders who ridiculed Him, and they saw Him tenderly touch lepers, people who were possessed by demons, the blind, and the sick. To be sure, His disciples were pretty slow on the uptake, but they eventually absorbed Jesus's heart and values. But we're not living in first-century Palestine, and we can't hang out with Jesus. Is it possible for us have Him imprinted on our lives? Absolutely. In Paul's letter to the Ephesians, he made the connection between God's heart and ours:

> Get rid of all bitterness, rage, anger, harsh words, and slander, as well as all types of evil behavior. Instead, be kind to each other, tenderhearted, forgiving one another, just as God through Christ has forgiven you.
>
> Imitate God, therefore, in everything you do, because

you are his dear children. Live a life filled with love, following the example of Christ. He loved us and offered himself as a sacrifice for us, a pleasing aroma to God. (Ephesians 4:31–5:2 NLT)

As we imitate God, we'll realize we have very ungodly things in our hearts—bitterness, rage, anger, and so on. When we experience God's forgiveness for our sins, we're capable and motivated to forgive those who offend us. And we'll go beyond forgiving them to actually loving them, like Jesus did, even when they don't love us in return. This doesn't mean we should become vulnerable to abusers. Those who are in a dangerous relationship (physically or emotionally) should protect themselves, but as they increasingly experience God's forgiveness and love, they won't hate the abuser any longer.

In another letter, Paul asked people to imprint on him as he followed Jesus. The letter to the Philippians is a thank-you note for their help in his ministry. They had seen him cast a demon out of a young girl, preach, be thrown in prison, and get rescued by an earthquake sent by God. He had impressed them, for sure! Now, he told them:

Dear brothers and sisters, one final thing. Fix your thoughts on what is true, and honorable, and right, and pure, and lovely, and admirable. Think about things that are excellent and worthy of praise. Keep putting into practice all you learned and received from me—everything you heard from me and saw me doing. Then the God of peace will be with you. (Philippians 4:8–9 NLT)

Paul was telling the Philippians and believers of today to watch him. To learn what he learned, believe what he believed, do what he did . . . and experience the presence of the God of peace. Is it presumptuous to ask our kids to follow us like that? No, because they're already doing it! The more poignant questions for us as parents are, "What do they hear *in our talk?*" and "What do they see *in our walk?*"

You teach what you know, you reproduce who you are.

—JACK FROST

IN OUR TALK

We may think our children aren't listening when we're having conversations while they ride in the back seat, but they hear more than we imagine. Experts tell us that words make up only 7 percent of all communication; the rest is the tone of voice and gestures. So even if our actual words aren't poisonous, we can have a very negative impact on those listening by the way we say them.

A friend of ours said that when his son was about eight years old, the boy was riding his bike near him and hit a bump in the pavement. Instantly, the boy muttered, "Damn!"

His dad was surprised. He asked, "Where did you hear that word?"

The reply was immediate and crushing: "From you."

In Paul's letter to the Ephesians he challenges them (and now us) to be life-giving with our words: "Don't use foul or abusive language. Let everything you say be good and helpful, so that your words will be an encouragement to those who hear them" (Ephesians 4:29 NLT). That's a high standard, but it's how we correct our communication to be sweet, positive, and encouraging for those who are listening to us. This doesn't mean we can't say hard things to correct people, but we'll say them with kindness and hope, not to punish or manipulate.

IN OUR WALK

We're convinced that very little escapes the notice of children. They may not understand how to interpret every event, but they're watching every moment. What do they see? They're especially interested when they see:

- How we respond to failure: Do we blame someone else, deny the event even happened, minimize it by saying, "It's no big deal," or excuse ourselves with, "I couldn't help it"? Or do we model what it looks like to take responsibility, admit our part in the failure, and find the seed of growth to nurture for the future?

- What matters to us: We can say that God is most important to us or that our family is our priority, but is that what our kids see in action? Too often, the priorities we impart are our thirst for success, power, pleasure, and approval. If these are the things we talk most about—the things that make our eyes light up and our voices become more intense, and what we complain about when they don't happen—our behavior has sent a loud and clear message to our kids.

- How we relate to our spouses: We've heard it said that the best gift we can give our kids is for men to love their wives. It's also true that a great gift to children is for wives to respect their husbands . . . and for both to show these things often and well. In broken homes, parents are tempted to disparage their former partners. Their deep hurt and resentment spill out and make a powerful impression on the kids. Be careful to communicate at least some degree of respect for one another, unless, of course, you need a restraining order or some other means of protecting yourself and your children.

- How we spend our money: Few choices have as much impact on our kids as how we use money. Does the desire for more control us, or are we content with what we have? Have we spent beyond our means until we're drowning in debt and worrying about it constantly? Or are we wise, careful in our spending, and joyful in our generosity? A friend told us that his mother constantly worried about money. Her father grew up in very hard times, so no matter how much money she had in the bank, she learned from him that it was never enough. Is that what we want our kids to pick up from us? Finding contentment in small things, time spent together doing free things, and teaching our kids good financial lessons will impart the right message about money.

- How we invest our time: Time is a precious commodity that can be invested or wasted. Today, electronic devices have been almost implanted in our hands and in our ears, and many of us live lives dominated by screen time. There's nothing wrong with using the latest tools to learn and communicate—unless they consume all of our time. We're wise to evaluate how much time we're spending in activities that interfere with good communication with one another. We probably need to make some hard decisions about phones, computers, tablets, and the television. Change will probably be hard, especially for those who are most invested in these devices, but soon the benefits of knowing each other better will be obvious.

After Richard graduated from college with a degree in mechanical engineering, he took a job with one of the major oil companies. He worked at a plant in Texas for several years to learn the ropes. He and Alicia had gotten married when they were in college, and within a few years, they had a son and a daughter. Richard and some of those who graduated with him realized there was a proven path to promotions in the company. They met people who had been assigned to jobs all over the nation and in foreign countries. The track to success and the big salaries was being open to relocation, but Richard had other ideas about what gives meaning to success. Though his employer offered him promotions again and again, he only took the ones that allowed his family to stay where they were. Others climbed much higher and made a lot more money, but Richard had done the cost-benefit analysis and concluded that his family was more important than those things. He was radically committed to avoiding drift in his family's relationships.

Today, Richard is retired from the oil company. Sometimes, he feels a little sad when he hears from former colleagues about their homes in the mountains or on the beach, but not *that* sad. He looks at the life he provided for his son and daughter, who now have families of their own, and he's very grateful he had the good sense to choose his family over his career. He invested his time and his heart where it matters most.

What you put first will be what you are at the last.

—BRIAN HOUSTON

CONNECTING WITH GOD'S FAMILY

A few decades ago, a "regular church attender" was someone who came to services almost every Sunday out of the year. In recent years, a regular church attender was reidentified as someone who came to church three out of four Sundays a month, and, shockingly, today, regular attendance is defined as showing up once or twice a month. The trend is clear. The problem isn't about filling seats; it's about what we value, what we pursue, what we sacrifice, and what our choices are saying to our kids.

A study by LifeWay Research reveals the impact of parents on their children's spiritual development:

1. When both parents attend small group Bible studies (also known as Sunday school or house church) in addition to the Sunday service, 72% of their children attend small group Bible studies when grown.
2. When only the father attends a small group Bible study, 55% of the children attend when grown.
3. When only the mother attends a small group Bible study, 15% of the children attend when grown.
4. When neither parent attends a small group Bible study, only 6% of the children attend when grown.

The impact of fathers is especially profound. When a young person becomes a Christian, there's only a 3.5 percent probability that the rest of the family will trust in Christ. If the mother is the first to believe in Jesus, there's a 17 percent probability that the rest will follow. But when the father is the first to believe, there is a 93 percent probability the rest of the family will follow Christ.[4] As pastors for nearly thirty years, here is what we (Rodney and Michelle) know to be true—parents who treat the church as optional shouldn't be surprised when their children treat Jesus as unnecessary.

One of the main complaints of young people is that the adults they see in church live double lives—and quite often, they're talking about their parents. They see the adults sing worship songs on Sunday, but they then act devoid of kindness, love, and honesty the rest of the week. We make a big mistake if we tell them they're wrong. Defensiveness only affirms their perceptions and drives them away. Instead, we need to invite dialogue, letting them give us their perceptions without defying them, correcting them, or interrupting them. We need to learn those powerful and rare words that are too seldom used in tense conversations: "Tell me more of what you're thinking." And then we need to keep listening.

We can be honest about the disconnect on the part of many people. In fact, to some extent all of us are hypocrites because we don't live up to the standards of true godliness. But our kids aren't looking for perfection. They're looking for honesty. If we can find the courage to admit when our actions don't match our stated beliefs, we'll open doors of meaningful communication that can last for the rest of our lives.

Encourage your kids to ask any question and share every opinion. They may push back on some of the basics of the faith. Don't overreact! Keep your composure and say, "Tell me more." Don't think that you have to get them to the "right answer" in the first conversation . . . or in any conversation. If your kids are thinking, they'll explore the foundations of what they believe. It's part of growing up, not a character flaw. In fact, if a growing adolescent never voices concerns or questions about the important things of life, we should be worried!

YOUR TURN

In this book, we've explored the importance of establishing a personal and family mission (Why do we exist?), crafting a set of values (What do we care about?), and identifying the vision (Where are we going?). Now it's time to consider the strategy, asking "How will we get there?" You'll need a plan, and you'll need to refine the plan from time to time. The plan is about putting your intentions on paper so they're crystal clear and you know the process to reach your goals.

A company CEO can write these elements with the input of the management team or board, and parents (including single parents) have a similar privilege and responsibility of leading the family to articulate a plan to achieve common goals. We suggest taking about thirty days to work through identifying what your mission, vision, and values will be as a family. It may take longer, and that's perfectly okay. The time spent isn't important; the quality of how you spend that time is.

You can follow the *shift* acronym to guide your conversations. Start with the end in mind. Discuss who you want to become as a family. Paint a verbal picture of what you're striving for. Start with open-ended questions that allow everyone to articulate what their ideal family would look like. Discuss the specific purpose your family is going to fulfill. Allow that purpose to define your mission. Decide what the nonnegotiables are going to be. What will be important to you and how are you going to behave as a family? If age appropriate, have everyone work through the Family Goal Tree discussed in chapter 7 and brainstorm ways you can work together and hold one another accountable to achieve those goals. Again, depending on the age and stage of each family member you can take as much time as necessary so that everyone sees the benefit and value of working through these critical steps for long-term success as a family. This should be something the family sees as a blessing and benefit rather than a burden. The goal is to make this a fun and memorable experience.

When our girls were in middle school and Luke was in elementary school, we had our first family conversation about our mission, vision, and values. They were old enough to offer their opinions, and they were thrilled that we valued their input. We didn't use words that sounded like they came from corporate boardrooms. Instead, we used memorable, easily understood terms. The process of articulating these concepts together gave our family a strong sense of identity and ownership. We defined what we wanted to be known for. I (Michelle) found a decal at Hobby Lobby that perfectly describes our mission and vision as a family. It was in a beautiful script font with the Bible verse found in Joshua 24:15: "But as for me and my family, we will serve the LORD" (NLT). We wanted everyone who walked in and out of our home, including ourselves, to be reminded of our mission and vision as a family. We realized how each of us uniquely contributes to the success of the others, and together, we had a sense of destiny.

As you talk to your family, share your convictions about what's most important to you, and invite the input of everyone in the family. Take the long view—don't expect quick, simple answers to life's most significant issues. Encourage dialogue, study, talk some more, and have deeper conversations. Sooner or later, you'll have a plan to pursue what matters most—how you relate to each other, how you spend your money, and how you invest your time.

This is where the proverbial rubber meets the road. A few of us are instinctive and don't seem to need much planning, but the rest of us need a clear, compelling plan that captures our hearts and gives us a track to run on. Create a plan that works for you and your family. Have a blend of tenacity and flexibility, and realize that each person in your family may need something different to keep them motivated. Some need structure, some need room for creativity, and some need more encouragement than others. Be a student of your family. Take the time to craft this plan, and watch how God uses you to inspire the people you love.

 THINK ABOUT IT:

1. What values, attitudes, and behaviors did you absorb from your parents?
2. Did you copy them or react in an opposite way? Explain your answer.

3. What do your children hear and what do they pick up in nonverbal cues when they hear you talk? How do you know?
4. How are you modeling a response to failure?
5. Are you modeling the values that matter most to you?
6. What do your kids see in your relationship with your spouse (or your ex)?
7. If your kids follow your example about time and money, where will it lead them?
8. What can you do to let them see an authentic relationship with God and with God's people in the church?

 DO IT:

1. With your spouse, take some time to think, pray, and plan your strategy to intentionally implement the changes you've identified from previous chapters and lessons learned here.
2. Share your plans with your children. Value their questions and engage them in conversations about how your family will live out your values.

CHAPTER 13

THE POWER OF UNCONDITIONAL LOVE

Extend Forgiveness and Mercy Consistently

The best use of life is love.
The best expression of love is time.
The best time to love is now.

—RICK WARREN

I (Rodney) would like to say I'm the paragon of virtue when it comes to responding to my children's misbehavior through the years with calmness and wisdom, but I'm still on the learning curve. I think I did pretty well with my daughters Becca and Ashlyn, but with Luke, as he grew older, the testosterone levels kicked in from both of us. I'm afraid I went overboard sometimes. I learned that when I raised my voice, Luke raised his! Far too often, I respond by raising mine again, and he would follow my lead. The unspoken but very real question we were both asking was, "Who's going to win this shouting match?" My assumption was that since I'm the dad, I should win. I learned that Luke didn't always make that assumption!

As you can imagine, our "conversations" didn't turn out well. After several rounds of escalation, Luke would walk off and go to his room. We would both stew for a while—long enough for me to feel guilty for not having enough self-control and empathy. I would regret things I said and how I said them, but instead of letting the anger and guilt take root, I would take the steps toward Luke's room, knock on the door, and ask him to forgive me for losing it. I would always tell him that it was wrong of me to lose my cool, and I would always reassure him of my love for him. You would have to know Luke's personality to appreciate this, but every time, he would look at me smiling and say, "Yeah, Dad. I know you love me." I'd walk away relieved that my relationship with my son was restored this time, but I often wondered how I let that eruption of anger happen . . . again . . . and again.

We're steeped in a culture that talks a lot about love but seldom understands it beyond a superficial level. In describing love between a man and a woman, the messages are all about hot romance and tender feelings. And in parents' relationships with their kids, it seems that love means giving them everything they could ever want. If we're not careful, we won't just drift—we'll be swept downstream in the culture's torrent! It helps if we start on or get back on the right track by trying to understand the nature of love.

To love someone means to see him
as God intended him to be.
—FYODOR DOSTOEVSKY

CONSUMER OR COMMITTED?

There are two kinds of relationships: *consumer* relationships and *committed* relationships. The two are miles apart. Most of the connections we have are the consumer type. The question we inherently ask is, "What's best for me?" As long as the relationship meets our needs, we'll stay, but when something better comes along, we drop one and pick up the other. My (Michelle's) relationship with the salesperson at a clothing boutique is like this: If she can sell me a fabulous dress at a good price, I'll probably go back to buy another outfit from her . . . unless I see an ad from another store with a more enticing offer. Where we shop for clothes, groceries, fast food, internet services, and how we choose between virtually every brick and mortar store or online store are determined by what options best meet our needs. In these cases, our needs are more important than the relationship.

That's all fine and reasonable when we're thinking about buying a cup of coffee, but it doesn't work in our most important relationships. Obviously, our kids are not products, they're people. If we're not careful, we can bring a consumer mindset into our relationships with our kids. When they excel in sports or make great grades in school, we feel proud because their success reflects our great parenting—or that's what we want others to conclude. But when they aren't too gifted in athletics, academics, choosing friends, or in physical appearance, we feel embarrassed. And we don't like feeling embarrassed! To solve the problem, we put pressure on our kids to perform better. We say it's for their sake so they'll excel later in life—and we're sure there's some of that motivation in the mix, but most of the pressure we put on our kids is because their performance and appearance aren't meeting *our* needs or expectations. No, we don't plan to ditch them and find other kids to bring home, but we sure wish they'd do a better job of reflecting our high standards of excellence!

As parents, we can't ever allow our love and acceptance to be determined by our children's performance. I'm thankful that God's love for us is not based upon our performance. If that were the case we wouldn't have any hope because it would be impossible to please Him. However, I'm thankful that God loves us unconditionally and He accepts us not based upon what we do but who we are— His creation.

Love is a decision. It's also a commitment in which the relationship is more important than our needs. Instead of asking, "What's best for me?" here, people pursue what's best for the other person. We sacrifice for each other, not because we have to, but because we cherish the other. Only a few relationships rise to this kind of commitment: marriage, parenting our children, our relationship with God, and our spiritual family.

Another way to describe these strong, unbending relationships is with the word "covenant." Throughout the Bible, God makes covenants with people—from Adam to Noah to Abraham to Moses to the new covenant in Jesus. Some of these are conditional. God says, "I'll do this but you have to do that." But some are unconditional: "[I'll] never leave you nor forsake you" (Deuteronomy 31:6). The conditional ones challenge us, get our attention, and compel compliance, but the unconditional ones warm our hearts and inspire us to follow the One who has proclaimed His love for us. In our marriages and as we parent our children, our understanding of these covenant relationships gives us a firm foundation to love unconditionally. We've experienced the love, forgiveness, and acceptance of God, so we pour out love, forgiveness, and acceptance to the ones we love—even when it's inconvenient, even when they aren't meeting our needs, and even when they don't appreciate what we do for them.

THE DIFFERENCE

Men and women seem to speak different languages, and some have said they're from different planets! In Paul's letter to the Ephesians, he described the deep commitment husbands and wives have for each other. The relationship isn't for convenience or even for thrills. Instead, it's a picture of our relationship with God. He told husbands to love their wives "just as Christ loved the church" and "gave himself up" in sacrificial love. But he gave a different instruction to wives: to respect their husbands (Ephesians 5:21–33).

Dr. Emerson Eggerichs's study of married couples resulted in a fascinating discovery:

> We believe love best motivates a woman and respect most powerfully motivates a man. Research reveals that during marital conflict a husband most often reacts unlovingly when feeling disrespected, and a wife reacts disrespectfully when feeling unloved. We asked 7,000 people the question, "When you are in a conflict with your spouse or significant other, do you feel unloved or disrespected?" 83% of the men said "disrespected" and 72% of the women said "unloved." Though we all need love and respect equally, the felt need differs during conflict, and this difference is as different as pink is from blue![1]

It is wise for a husband to understand that the identity of his wife is tied to her work professionally as much as it is domestically as a wife and mother. Husbands can help their wives feel loved, supported, and appreciated by calling them during the day, offering to run errands, volunteering to change diapers or wash dishes, calling in dinner date reservations, and doing other things specific for their relationship. When men don't do things like this for their wives, the wives feels taken for granted and unappreciated. And each wife needs to realize her husband's identity is also, to a significant degree, tied up in his work, his intelligence, skills, and accomplishments. When she doesn't show confidence, give encouragement, and celebrate him it crushes him . . . and he may react with sarcasm, anger, or silence.

When wives feel adored and husbands feel honored, children have a safe place to grow and thrive. They see love in action in their parents' relationship, and they internalize the unique strength of a committed relationship. They may not be able to articulate the difference between a consumer relationship and a committed one, but they instinctively know the difference.

This isn't an academic exercise for children. They're dramatically affected by the type of relationship they see in the home. They'll look for friends who treat them with honor and speak the truth, and they'll look for a spouse who has these values. Then they'll instill their children with the values of a committed relationship, and the legacy is passed from generation to generation.

Our children are not going to be just "our children"—
they are going to be other people's husbands and wives
and the parents of our grandchildren.

—MARY S. CALDERONE

PAY IT FORWARD

We've had the privilege of watching a lot of amazing parents model love and respect to their kids. Here are some of the most important practices they've used:

Notice, name, and nurture strengths

It's so easy for us parents to become fixated on the misbehavior and flaws in our children that we find ourselves constantly correcting them. We need to become experts at finding the good and shining a spotlight on it in our kids. Notice your kids' successes—and even their progress toward success. Put a label on the strengths they display so these words become a part of your children's identity, and then provide resources to help your children excel in those areas.

A friend's son showed remarkable promise in art from the time he was only four or five years old. In fact, he began drawing in perspective when he was five. His dad, by his own admission, is artistically backward, and could have squashed his son's talents because he was uncomfortable with his son having a talent he didn't have himself. But, luckily, he quickly realized his son had a gift that needed to be developed. He bought his son plenty of art supplies, had great conversations with him about his drawings, and became his biggest cheerleader. Throughout his school years, the young man honed his talents. He majored in fine art in college, and today makes a good living as an illustrator.

Invest time and affection

Raising strong, confident children is as much an art as it is a science, but two things are absolutely necessary: time and tenderness. Some have insisted that our kids need only "quality time," but in the experience of thousands of parents I know, the only way to have quality time is to have quantity time. In many ways, love is still synonymous with time. Yes, we're busy. Yes, many of us work long hours. I'd say that we need to make sure our priorities are aligned with God's. If we have to work overtime for a season, that's no big deal, but if we've made our careers more important than our children, we will pay a steep price for it down the road—at the expense of being involved in our children's lives.

Meaningful touch is just one way of showing affection to our kids, but it's one of the best. Even young men don't shake off a hug or a hand on their backs with a smile that says, "You mean the world to me!"

Be a good forgiver

Many of us aren't good at forgiveness—whether giving or receiving. The best we can do is get to a point where we tolerate the person who has offended us, but that's certainly not the same thing as offering genuine forgiveness. When people wrong us, they create a debt: they owe us. We can eliminate the debt in one of two ways—either we make them pay the debt or we pay it. If someone comes into your house and breaks a vase, either that person will pay for another one, you'll buy a new one, or you'll do without one. In one way or another, someone will pay for it. In forgiveness, we're taking the step of paying the debt down ourselves. For small offenses, we can absorb the loss pretty quickly, but for abuse or betrayal, the process takes a while.

How do we know if we've forgiven people who've hurt or wronged us? One of the surest ways is to analyze our thoughts about them. Do we secretly (or not so secretly) delight when we hear they're having problems? Are we glad when we hear someone else talk about their faults? Do we daydream about them suffering for what they've done?

We can be good forgivers only to the extent of understanding how much God has forgiven us. Our debt was paid by Jesus—fully and for all time. In John 19:30 we find the last words He spoke on the cross before He died were: "It is finished." Out of a heart overflowing with the gratitude of being forgiven, we can forgive those who have hurt us.

Our children see revenge and retaliation every day at school. Do they see something else at home? Of course, this extends immediately to the way we respond to our kids when they disobey. We forgive them, and our love always wants the best for them, so as we forgive, we hold them accountable. In this, we give them correction without condemnation. We don't call them names, we don't snarl, we don't turn and walk away in disgust, and we don't continually call attention to the offense or wrong. Instead, we can say, "Son, I forgive you. Now, what will you do next time?" For some of us, this kind of response is easy because that's the way our parents treated us, but for many, this is a foreign language! We've never seen it, we've never known it was possible, and we're starting in the hole. But it's still possible even for those of us who are new to the experience of forgiveness. We can admit our tendency to carry a grudge, focus on the forgiveness Christ has given us in abundance, and practice saying, "I forgive you. What will you do next time?"

Incorporate the three c's: Be calm, be clear, and enforce consequences

One of the main reasons parents have conflicts with their kids is that they don't communicate clear expectations, and even when they do, they don't follow through on the consequences. This confuses children and makes them assume we don't really care. And when they make this assumption, we get angry and defensive . . . and more demanding. Ever been there? We (Rodney and Michelle) certainly have. Even when we're clear about our expectations, we can expect teenagers to push the boundaries.

When Becca was in high school, she developed a friendship with a boy in her class. We thought he was just one of the large group of friends she hung out with, but at one point we discovered they had moved past friendship to infatuation. She knew he wasn't on the "Approved for Dating" list (if there had been one), so she had tried to hide their relationship. Rodney and I (Michelle) were pretty upset.

The boy was very popular and charming . . . actually, too charming. When he showed interest in Becca, she was thrilled. However, he didn't have the best reputation when it came to his track record with girls—a fact that Becca either didn't know or chose to ignore but Rodney and I knew based on comments and concerns that had gotten back to us from other parents. When we told Becca that we didn't want her to be around him, she became furious. She accused us of overreacting and judging him unfairly. I explained that we knew of his reputation, and we didn't want her to get hurt. She stormed off to her room and slammed the door. Rodney called the boy to let him know that their relationship was over and we didn't want him to pursue Becca anymore. It wasn't that he was a bad kid or a trouble-maker, but because of the reputation that had preceded him, we knew his values were not in alignment with the values of our family.

We loved Becca too much to let her stay in a relationship that potentially could cause her to drift. Of course, she insisted that we needed to trust her, but we remained firm in our assessment of the boy's reputation. Thankfully, over a few weeks, Becca realized what we'd said about the boy was true, and she understood why we had set such a hard boundary about their relationship. It proved to be a very positive experience for her because she realized her infatuation could have led to choices she would have later regretted.

Parenting is a delicate balance of convincing your child they can do anything in life while simultaneously screaming "Don't do that!" every three minutes.

—DAVID CRANK

It's been said that parenting is simple but it's not easy. Raising children is one of the greatest joys and one of the greatest responsibilities in life. In our own experiences, we have learned that there are three *c*'s essential for good parenting, healthy relationships, and real growth in a child's character. First, be *calm*. Far too often, we interpret every disagreement or delay in our children's obedience as a personal offense. Whether they mean it this way or not, we need to refuse to light the fuse! Stay calm. Take a deep breath, maybe walk around for a few minutes, and when you're ready, come back to speak with self-control to your child (and anyone else within earshot).

Second, you need to set very *clear* and age-appropriate expectations: We don't set a curfew for a toddler. Part of the art of parenting is to determine what is a reasonable expectation for children at each stage of development, including things like how they manage their rooms, household chores, homework, money, relationships, how they interact with video games, particular websites, and on and on. We would recommend that you don't give your child, at any age, a manual of all the demands of the household. Children follow plenty of rules at school, and may resent having even more rules at home. Expectations and restrictions should be shared out of love for your child's safety and well-being—not out of being a gatekeeper. Keep it as simple and clear as possible. When these rules and expectations become habits, add another one or two.

Third, make sure the *consequences* are very clear, are reasonable, fit the offense, and are enforceable. If one day out of the blue you frustratingly say, "If you don't clean up your room, you'll be grounded and I'm taking your phone for a month," you'll likely lose credibility in two ways: you haven't matched the consequence with the offense, and you probably won't follow through with it anyway. This would only heighten frustrations all around. It's far better to have a dialogue with your children about the consequences, and even *let them determine* what sort of consequences are appropriate for their actions or nonactions. Quite often, they'll be stricter than you are, and you may need to ratchet them back a bit.

By all means, follow through with the consequences. You can adjust them next time if they're too light or too strong, but do what you promised you'd do—especially if the child has established the expectation and consequences.

Let's repeat: through it all, be calm and kind. We're the grown-ups in the room, and we need to act like it. Yes, there are times when we want to scream . . . times when we're at the end of our ropes and we don't think we can take it anymore. In the PBS documentary, *Baseball*, Dick Stockton describes the self-control of Pittsburgh Pirates slugger Willie Stargell in the 1975 World Series. Willie had led the League in runs batted in that year. However, he could hardly do anything in the World Series. He popped up and struck out almost every time at bat. Yet, he never complained. He never said anything as he walked back to the dugout. He never threw his bat down. After the series, Dick went up to him and asked, "How can you keep your composure? You must be dying." Willie's answer stunned Dick. Willie's little boy, Wilver Jr., was playing in the locker room. Willie made a gesture toward him and said, "The time comes when a man really has to be a man."[2]

Willie Stargell could have thrown his bat, cursed, and stomped around the dugout or the clubhouse, but he realized the model he provided for his little boy was more important than his baseball reputation. "The time comes when a man really has to be a man" . . . what an example we can lead with as parents!

KEEP FILLING THE TANK

Dr. Ross Campbell has a powerful illustration for parents. In *How to Really Love Your Child*, he says that it's our job to fill, and keep filling, the "emotional tank" in our kids:

> This tank is figurative, of course, but nevertheless is real. Each child has certain emotional needs, and whether these emotional needs are met (through love, understanding, discipline, and so on) determines many things. First of all, it determines how a child feels: whether the child is content,

angry, depressed, or joyful. Second, it affects behavior: whether the child is obedient, disobedient, whiny, perky, playful, or withdrawn. Naturally, the fuller the emotional tank, the more positive feelings and the better the behavior.[3]

Are we filling their tanks or depleting them? If our children are in school, they probably come home many days with their emotional tanks bone dry. At every age, they need our love, our words of hope and affirmation, and our faith that they have a bright future. We fill their tanks with our words, our touch, our smiles, our confidence, and our time. When their tanks are low, we can step up and fill them— even when we're tired, even when we're busy, and even when we'd rather be somewhere else. That's what it means to love our children unconditionally. And you'll likely be surprised that when you share your love with your child, your own emotional tank starts to fill back up too. The simple ways your child displays love for you will certainly lift you up even on the most draining of days.

One of the very practical things my (Rodney's) father did for my brothers and me is that he made a point of introducing us to people he respected. They were prominent athletes, political leaders, or gifted speakers, and all of them had won my father's heart— usually because they had overcome incredible odds to achieve success. Meeting them filled my emotional tank because I felt included in my dad's world, and these people inspired me to dream bigger and reach higher.

One summer my dad invited me to serve as an intern in his outreach events held in different cities across the country. That was the first time I really understood and learned to appreciate my father's ministry, where God used him to affect so many people's lives. That summer propelled me to imagine how God might use me too. I saw how God could use me in the lives of young people, and my sense of passion became much clearer and stronger. But it doesn't stop with me. Exposing our three children to outstanding people is one of the ways Michelle and I are trying to fill their emotional tanks and lift them higher. We always look for opportunities to introduce our kids to people who are making a difference and especially those who have overcome obstacles to get there. We always believed they would benefit from being around other great leaders and people of influence. We believed it would serve as fuel for their confidence and vision for their futures.

Vision can't be taught, it must be caught.

—FREDDIE GAGE

As parents we have to remember that one of the great responsibilities we have is to create an atmosphere in our home and to establish a relationship with our children that is like freshly poured cement. We only have a short amount of time with them before the cement hardens. Now is the time to make a lasting, positive impression on the wet cement of our children's hearts and lives before it's too late.

 THINK ABOUT IT:

1. How would you describe the differences between a consumer relationship and a committed relationship?
2. How can you tell which kind you have in your marriage? With your children?

3. Why is it important to understand that, in general, wives thrive when they feel loved and husbands thrive when they feel respected?

4. What are your children's strengths? How can you affirm them and provide resources for them to excel in these areas?

5. Are you a good forgiver? If you have work to do on forgiving others more completely, what do you need to be able to forgive from your heart?

6. After reading the section on setting expectations and enforcing consequences, do you need to make any changes with your kids? If so, describe your first steps.

7. What are some ways you can fill the emotional tanks of your children today? What difference will it make for your family?

 DO IT:

1. Make a list of people you admire, especially those who have overcome great obstacles.

2. Make an appointment to take at least one of your children to meet one of them, or have the person come to your house for dinner or just a conversation. Afterward, talk to your family about the courage the person displayed.

CHAPTER 14

LEAVING THE NEST

Raise Them and Release Them

Part of the thrill of guiding children into adulthood
is the release. But it's also a parent's greatest act of
surrender. Still, you have to let them go. Start now.

—CHUCK SWINDOLL

I n over twenty years raising our own children and working with
hundreds of other families, we (Rodney and Michelle) have concluded that parents need to give their kids two things: roots and
wings. Roots of security and wisdom and wings of confidence to soar
as adults. Sadly, not all parents provide these twin necessities.

Some provide roots without wings. We've watched young people
who have been smothered by well-meaning parents leave for college
or their careers without the confidence or skills necessary for success. Their parents thought they were helping by giving their kids
everything they needed and making their decisions for them, but the
result was that their children were more like toddlers than adults.

They were impulsive or indecisive (sometimes at the same time), and were often confused because they hadn't developed the skills of analysis and decision-making. Sometimes the parents want their grown children to remain dependent on them. I know parents who call their kids in college *every* day, and even worse, their kids feel the need to call home every day!

We've also seen some young adults struggle because their parents were physically or emotionally detached, and the kids had to figure things out on their own. Their parents gave them wings of independence but very shallow roots. Sometimes, the parents' preoccupation was due to something out of their control, like their own health crises or critical problems with another person in the family, and their attention was absorbed by the drama. But some parents are so fixated on their own careers (or hobbies) that they essentially abandon their families emotionally. Without strong relationships at home, some young adults become fiercely self-reliant, but some gravitate to anyone who will pay attention to them—sometimes with disastrous effects. No one loved them, no one believed in them, so they spend the rest of their lives searching for affection and meaning. When they marry and have kids, they don't have a clue about how to relate to them, and the cycle often continues.

Without roots, kids drift. Without wings, they won't shift.
—RODNEY AND MICHELLE GAGE

But we've also watched wise parents build character and life skills into their children. They didn't wait until the day before their kids were leaving home. They began the process when they were very young, and over about eighteen years of teaching, training, modeling, and countless events of trial and error, their children gradually acquired what they needed to make a difference in the world, make hard decisions, and build strong relationships.

The goal of parenting isn't to make our kids permanently dependent on us; it's to give them what they need to be healthy, independent, creative, loving adults. Roots *and* wings. Psychologist Charleen Alderfer explains the importance of both:

A healthy family provides a secure environment for growth and learning. There is a sense of "we-ness" and belonging on the part of each member. There are fair limits that are understandable and discussable. There are boundaries that protect members and boundaries that expand to let in new members and new information. There is a sense of loyalty that is strong and does not impede one from developing into a person with individual ideas, dreams, and behavior. Humor in a family improves its general health and well-being. There is no question that the way a family functions will define, to a large measure, how well a child will develop.

Roots—a knowledge of belonging, and wings—a recognition of the need for autonomy; these together are what children need from their families to become productive, well-functioning and happy adults.[1]

BEGIN WITH THE END IN MIND

It's never too early to think, plan, and pray about launching our kids into their adult lives. If our goal is to give them security and confidence, we'll start when they're little to impart the concepts of independence. Actually, we're not alone in our goal. God has created us to separate—to *individuate*, to use a psychologist's term—from our parents.[2] We see this most dramatically in two of the stages of development: at about two years old and in adolescence. When children turn two, they begin to find their own voices, their own desires, and their own possessions. They have been very dependent on their parents, especially their mothers, but now they pull away. They stomp their little feet and say, "No!" to every question or instruction. They didn't suddenly become demon-possessed! They're just taking the first steps toward finding their own identities apart from their parents.

Of course, the second stage of pulling away is adolescence. The combination of opportunities, peer pressure, and hormones have a powerful effect to drive teens to separate from their parents. For some, no matter what the parents think about any topic, the teenager disagrees. A few remain compliant, but most push boundaries. They experiment with ideas, people, and goals. This isn't abnormal; it's completely normal. They're trying to establish themselves and figure out their place in the world.

Too often, parents interpret the pulling away during adolescence as a personal offense. They see every disagreement as a threat to what they hold dear and a blow to the values they've tried to instill in their kids. The teenager appears to be defiant and out of control . . . and in fact, may be defiant, but the teenager's attitude and behavior usually aren't as far out of bounds as the parents assume. Parents make things far worse by reacting so strongly and taking everything personally. For many of us, it's a very important shift to reframe what's going on with our teenagers . . . and see it as completely normal. If we understand the importance of this stage, we'll be their biggest cheerleaders instead of being perceived as prison guards.

Actually, our children's behavior does reflect on us. This fact can have opposite effects: We can either try to control and manipulate them, or we can love them well so they'll want to listen to our advice. The psalmist gave this insight about parenting:

Children are God's love-gift; they are heaven's generous reward. Children born to a young couple will one day rise to protect and provide for their parents. Happy will be the couple who has many of them! A household full of children will not bring shame on your name but victory when you face your enemies, for your offspring will have influence and honor to prevail on your behalf! (Psalm 127:3–5 TPT).

Let's leave our kids and grandkids more than just memories, let's leave them a legacy.

—RODNEY AND MICHELLE GAGE

DEEPER ROOTS, BROADER WINGS

It's the job of teenagers to create an identity that's separate from their parents. We can either support them as they work this out, or we can resist and resent them. We'll offer a few suggestions:

Develop a vision

At every stage of your child's development, use your imagination to envision how a son or daughter's personality and interests might translate into traits of a successful adult. Point to people, famous or familiar, who live remarkable lives. All of us need heroes; talk about the people who inspire you, and notice the ones that make your child's eyes widen. As you develop a vision for your child's future, remain open and flexible. God may have other plans, and your child may develop other interests, but having a sense of hope will be infectious.

When Becca was in college, she got a full scholarship for her singing, and she loved it. During the summer after her junior year, she became an intern at a large church in Birmingham, Alabama, and her heart was tugged toward ministry. The church was affiliated with another college, and they offered her a full scholarship, too. Since she was born, Rodney and I have communicated that we believed God had something special for her (just like we've communicated vision and destiny to Ashlyn and Luke). Now, Becca was torn between two incredible opportunities. Rodney and I sat down with her and talked through the pros and cons of each path based on her deepest, clearest, most compelling sense of passion. After a lot of discussion and prayer, she decided to leave the school she had been attending and enroll in the college in Birmingham. We're really proud of her for many reasons, but certainly one of them is that she has a mature decision-making process. We knew that either way she chose, she had a bright future, and God had great plans for her no matter what.

Prepare

The point of releasing children into the world, usually at about eighteen years old, requires preparation—of them and of us. One of our favorite quotes is by Zig Ziglar: "Success occurs when opportunity meets preparation."[3] For years, we guide, we equip, and we let them take more responsibility for their decisions so when the time comes, they feel excited and confident. A major part of preparing them for the future is letting them fail. Yes, we celebrate their successes, but we need to avoid protecting them too much from failure. When they were little, it was our responsibility to protect them because they were so vulnerable, but as they grow in their teen years, they need to develop wisdom, to choose friends wisely and to make good decisions. And one thing is certain: They'll fail at these things from time to time. Their failure may hurt us worse than it hurts them, but if we're too protective, they won't learn from their mistakes, and they won't gain the wisdom they desperately need to navigate the world away from home.

So . . . maybe we need to prepare ourselves as much as we prepare them. We need to be self-aware to know if *we're* making decisions *they* should be making and preventing them from learning the lessons that can only be learned from failure. If we realize we're too much of something—whether that be too involved or too hands-off—we can adjust. Quite often, husbands and wives are on opposite ends of this stick. If they can avoid seeing each other as "wrong," they can moderate each other and find a good balance. A lot depends on their communication. In our observations, a lot of parents are on the same page as long as their kids are little. The fireworks happen as children grow in responsibility and dependence, and the kids get caught in the middle. That's not good for anybody!

Do your homework. Read blogs and books, listen to podcasts about launching kids into adulthood. Seek out mentors and talk to people who have been down this road and learned the necessary lessons. And realize each child is different: One may go through this period smoothly, but a sibling may struggle with the complexity of pulling away while still staying connected.

The Scriptures give a powerful analogy about the principle of sowing and reaping. Like a farmer who gets tired, and maybe even discouraged, with all the work it takes before he sees the first signs of harvest, parents can lose heart. In his letter to the Galatians, Paul encouraged them, "Don't allow yourselves to be weary or disheartened in planting good seeds, for the season of reaping the wonderful harvest you've planted is coming!" (Galatians 6:9 TPT).

Encourage like crazy

People live for encouragement, and they die without it. Teenagers are especially vulnerable to self-doubt. Everything in their lives is up for grabs—relationships at home, relationships with friends, relationships with the opposite sex, and what the future holds, to name a few of their dilemmas. More than ever, they need us to look past their craziness (at least most of it) and give them what no one else on earth can give them: unconditional love.

As we discussed in an earlier chapter, there are three messages all young people need to hear: "I love you," "I'm proud of you," and "You're really good at this or that." We can use a variety of words to communicate these encouragements. They matter because, believe it or not, teenagers still look to their parents for support. We're like mirrors. When they look at us, do our faces say something affirming, or do they say something critical? Our words will be counterproductive if we don't mean them. When we're upset (and, at times, we will be—guaranteed), we should take some deep breaths and recalibrate our hearts so we can mean it when we say, "Hey, don't forget. No matter what happens, I love you so much. And I want you to know that I'm really proud to be your Mom (or Dad)." Do you think that'll make a difference? Of course it will.

Noticing and resourcing strengths will inspire and give a firm foundation for success. Teenagers, no matter how they look on the outside, are almost universally fragile on an emotional level. We can build confidence by describing how we can see their strengths having an impact on others. It's more than putting a label on their talents, which is important as a first step. We can provide much more encouragement as we see a bright future for them and describe it in some detail. Of course, a lot of pieces will be missing, and we won't be the ones to put those pieces in place, but a vision of the future seldom falls on deaf ears.

Guide appropriately

This is where parenting teenagers gets tricky. How much do we try to guide our children, and how much do we let them take the reins?

This isn't an easy question. The answer depends on a number of factors, such as the age and developmental stage of the child, personality and confidence, the level of our anxiety based on our own past mistakes, the opportunities in question, and the timing of decisions. The goal is to find a happy medium where you're not pushing and you're seen as an ally.

We (Rodney and Michelle) have taught our kids to trust God to open *and* close doors for them. We've tried to teach them that God's "no" is not a rejection. It's a redirection. They need to develop discernment to recognize the opportunities, obstacles, and just as important, the timing of their important decisions. One of the hardest things for any of us is waiting, so we've talked with Becca, Ashlyn, and Luke about the three answers to prayer. God may say "yes," He may say "no," and He may say "not now." The last one is often the most difficult to hear. God's delays aren't necessarily God's denials. In all of this, we realize it's important for them to make their own decisions. As they've matured, they've taken on more responsibility, and with that responsibility comes more confidence. We enjoy being their coaches and giving them input but letting them call the plays. They know they won't have the full picture of their future, but we encourage them to "do the next right thing" and trust that God will lead them to the next step and the next.

Discuss money
We believe one of the biggest failures of parents is not instilling practical perspectives about money into their kids. When they leave home, if they don't have good values and practices about money, they're a train wreck waiting to happen. Financial expert Dave Ramsey gives a lot of good advice to parents of adolescents, including:

- Show your kids how to make a budget. Work with them to list everything they buy, and help them develop a plan.

Make sure it's *their* budget, not yours for them. That's the only way they'll be motivated to follow it.

- Teach them the importance of setting long-range savings goals. If they're actually going to save, it's important for you to avoid buying them big-ticket items they really want. You may choose to provide matching funds for a car or something else that's very expensive, but don't make it too easy for them.
- No credit cards! Ramsey says, "Don't fill their brains with that 'you need a card to build your credit' crap. That's for people who want to make a life habit of borrowing money. Break that cycle before it even gets started by teaching them to not borrow."
- Expect the discipline of saving and spending on a budget to make a difference in other aspects of your teenager's life. Discipline, self-control, and delayed gratification are important traits in health, schoolwork, a career, and marriage.
- Ramsey concludes, "Love your kids enough to properly teach them about being adults. If they are deeply in debt with a marriage hanging by a thread in thirty years, what are you going to say? 'Sorry, son, that I didn't teach you better . . . but at least you thought I was cool when you were a teen!'"[4]

Another lesson to teach your kids regarding money is the importance of returning the tithe to God through your local church. We don't give *to* the church, we give *through* the church. In Leviticus 27:30 (NLT) the word *tithe* is translated as "one-tenth." If we teach our kids by example to give one-tenth out of every dollar they make, they'll always know they're living under God's umbrella of protection and provision. The tithe belongs to God, and when we're faithful in honoring God by returning what belongs to Him, God always provides for us, and in fact, He gives us more so we can be even more generous. We get to give, we don't give to get. Commit to making the shift in this area and watch what God will do. It's impossible to out-give God. If you don't believe it, read Malachi 3:10 and let God prove it to you!

Generosity is not a single act;
it is a way of seeing and thinking.
—BRIAN HOUSTON

Change roles

When your kids were very young, you were god-like: big, authoritative, and strong. As they got older and they learned to manage their growing autonomy, parenting became more like coaching. As they leave home, you're a trusted mentor. And later, when they have their careers and family, you're still their parent, but you become more of a peer. Don't be afraid of this transition. Embrace it—for their sakes and yours.

TRUST GOD

We're not on our own as we help our kids grow and thrive as young adults. We can trust God to guide us as much as we trust Him to guide them. We trust Him to lead them on the path He wants them to go. Jesus prayed, "Not my will, but yours be done" (Luke 22:42). That's our prayer for our kids: "Lord, I want what You want for them more than what I want for them . . . because You know far more than

I do!" God always leads people into and through times of struggle. Hard times don't necessarily mean our children are missing God's will. They may be right in the middle of it. We trust that He will teach them lessons they can only learn from trusting Him in good times and bad.

We trust God to use failure in their lives. We're not talking about accidents or other things that are out of their control. These are their personal mistakes. We have them, and they have them. When they happen, we trust they'll learn to be completely honest with God and honest with at least one other person—but maybe not us. And we hope God will show them more than ever the depth of His love and forgiveness so repentance brings them joy instead of shame.

We trust God to bless them with enough success and joy that they realize He is a wonderful Father who delights in them. And we trust God to correct them when they're getting off track. We trust God to bring people into their lives to encourage them and challenge them to be all they can be.

As we conclude our journey together, we want to say congratulations for getting this far! We've looked at five important shifts in this book. This last one, modeling a life of faith and integrity, will shape the lives of our children while they're with us and for the rest of their lives. Proverbs 22:6 says: "Dedicate your children to God and point them in the way that they should go, and the values they've learned from you will be with them for life" (TPT). This is our prayer for you.

Through the pages of this book, we have shared our hearts with you to give you hope and encouragement as you seek to live with greater intention. You have made one of the best investments you could ever make in yourself, your marriage, and in your family by reading this book. We have shared with you tools and resources to help you stop drifting. We walked you through a 5-Step Plan to serve as an ongoing support system to remind you of your mission, vision, and values as a couple and family. We've looked at the importance of identifying your goals, passions, and struggles to serve as motivation to fulfill your family's divine destiny. And, we've concluded with one of the greatest challenges of all, and that is to teach by example everything we have discussed. We believe in you, we are for you, and we declare that your best days are ahead of you.

Have you made the shift? If not, it's time.

 THINK ABOUT IT:

1. The goal of parenting is to give our children what they need to be healthy, independent, creative, loving adults. Do you agree or disagree with that statement?

2. How do some parents get it wrong? What are some of the results?

3. Describe the ways your parents gave you roots and wings. How could they have done it better?

4. What is your vision for your children? Why does having one matter?

5. What impact do we have on our kids when we communicate, "I love you," "I'm proud of you," and "You're really good at [a particular skill]"?

6. What are some ways you can help your children have a healthy concept of money?

7. What is your level of anxiety or confidence that your kids will become strong, responsible, loving adults?

DO IT:

1. Identify which of the five shifts in this book is most important to you.
2. Answer and discuss these questions as a family:
   - What difference will it make when you implement your most important shift?
   - What will be your three next steps to apply the principles in this book?

ACKNOWLEDGMENTS

Writing a book is like taking a trip. There is a lot of planning and preparation that goes into a book project. However, it's not about the destination or final product as much as it is about the people who share the journey with you. We (Rodney and Michelle) have had the joy of sharing this journey with some amazing people. First and foremost, we want to say a big thank you to Jana Burson, our literary agent, for believing in us and supporting us every step along the way. We also want to say thank you to Pat Springle and Stan Campbell for helping us craft and organize the Family Shift core message into what it has become. A big thank you to our church family at ReThink Life Church for their prayers, encouragement, standing with us, and for being a part of this journey. Lastly, we want to say thank you to Leeanna Nelson, our amazing editor, along with the entire team at Worthy Publishing for believing in us and helping us share this message to give hope and encouragement to families everywhere. It really does take teamwork to make the dream work.

NOTES

Chapter 1

1. Barna Group, "Forming Family Values in a Digital Age," Barna, June 27, 2017, https://www.barna.com/research/forming-family-values-digital-age/.

2. Cathy Lynn Grossman, "Americans Don't Cite 'God, Family, Country' Quite Like the Cliche Goes," *Washington Post*, March 20, 2015, https://www.washingtonpost.com/national/religion/americans-dont-cite-god-family-country-quite-like-the-cliche-goes/2015/03/20/bc3e0656-cf1b-11e4-8730-4f473416e759_story.html?noredirect=on&utm_term=.f1d915ffcc70.

3. John C. Maxwell in David McGowan, "Overcoming the Law of Diminishing Intent," greaterleadershipexcellence.com, January 15, 2018, http://greaterleadershipexcellence.com/2018/01/15/overcoming-the-law-of-diminishing-intent/.

Chapter 2

1. Andy Stanley (@AndyStanley), Twitter, April 17, 2013, https://twitter.com/andystanley/status/324713440541290498.

2. Monty Roberts, *The Man Who Listens to Horses* (Toronto: Vintage Canada, 1999), 98–100.

3. Roberts, 176–178.

4. Ed Young, *The Creative Leader: Unleashing the Power of Your Creative Potential* (Nashville: B&H Publishing, 2006), 131.

Chapter 3

1. John C. Maxwell, *The 21 Irrefutable Laws of Leadership: Follow Them and People Will Follow You* (Nashville: Thomas Nelson, 2007), 113.

2. Sarah Gardner, "Study Focuses on Strategies for Achieving Goals, Resolutions," Dominican University, https://www.dominican.edu/dominicannews/study-highlights-strategies-for-achieving-goals.

Chapter 4

1. "Everything You Need to Know about Wheel Alignment," *Completely Firestone* (blog), August 22, 2016, https://blog.firestonecompleteautocare.com/alignment/everything-you-need-to-know-about-wheel-alignment/.

2. Les and Leslie Parrott, "The Secret to Growing Together," Drs. Les and Leslie Parrott (website), August 20, 2013, www.lesandleslie.com/devotions/the-secret-to-growing-together/.

3. David Foster Wallace, "This Is Water," Kenyon College, May 21, 2005, transcript, http://bulletin-archive.kenyon.edu/x4280.html.

4. Michael Hyatt, *Your Best Year Ever* (Grand Rapids: Baker Books, 2018), 86.

5. Craig Groeschel, "Creating a Value-Driven Culture, Part 1," *Craig Groeschel Leadership Podcast*, Open Network, https://open.life.church/training/343-craig-groeschel-leadership -podcast-creating-a-value-driven-culture-part-1.

Chapter 5

1. Barna Group, "Morality Continues to Decay," Barna, November 3, 2003, https://www .barna.com/research/morality-continues-to-decay/.
2. George Barna in Barna Group, "Morality Continues to Decay."
3. George Barna in Barna Group, "Morality Continues to Decay."
4. Kay and Milan Yerkovich, "How Childhood Experiences Impact Marriage Relationships," Focus on the Family, 2012, https://www.focusonthefamily.com/marriage/communication -and-conflict/how-childhood-experiences-impact-marriage-relationships.
5. Les and Leslie Parrott, *Relationships* (Grand Rapids: Zondervan, 1998), 82–83.

Chapter 6

1. Boris Groysberg et al., "The Leader's Guide to Corporate Culture," *Harvard Business Review*, January–February 2018, https://hbr.org/2018/01/the-culture-factor.
2. Sharon Jaynes, *The Power of a Woman's Words* (Eugene, OR: Harvest House Publishers, 2007), 59.
3. Tara Haelle, "How to Teach Children that Failure Is the Secret to Success," NPR, May 6, 2016, https://www.npr.org/sections/health-shots/2016/05/06/476884049/how-to -teach-children-that-failure-is-the-secret-to-success.
4. Zig Ziglar, *See You at the Top* (Gretna, LA: Pelican Publishing Company, 2000), 105.

Chapter 7

1. Charles R. Swindoll, *Strengthening Your Grip* (Brentwood, TN: Worthy Books, 2015), 227.
2. Michael Hyatt, *Free to Focus: A Total Productivity System to Achieve More by Doing Less* (Grand Rapids: Baker, 2019), 195.

Chapter 8

1. Craig Groeschel (@lifechurch), Twitter, February 4, 2019, https://twitter.com/lifechurch /status/1092513150333841409.
2. The descriptions of four benefits are adapted from "Reasons to Learn More about Your Personality Type," Kendra Cherry, verywellmind, last updated March 19, 2019, https: //www.verywellmind.com/reasons-to-learn-more-about-your-personality-type-4099388.

Chapter 9

1. C. S. Lewis, *The Problem of Pain* (New York: HarperCollins, 1996), 92.
2. Henry Cloud, *Necessary Endings: The Employees, Businesses, and Relationships That All of Us Have to Give Up in Order to Move Forward* (Grand Rapids: Zondervan, 2010), 15–16.

3. John R. Wooden, Bill Sharman, and Bob Seizer, *The Wooden-Sharman Method: A Guide to Winning Basketball* (New York: MacMillan, 1975), 120.

4. Reader's Digest Association, *Quotable Quotes* (New York: Reader's Digest Association, 1997), 41.

Chapter 10

1. Ed Young, "The Sway of They," from the series "Fool," May 20, 2018, www.EdYoung.com, recorded sermon, https://edyoung.com/sermons/the-sway-of-they/.

2. Chris Widener, *Jim Rohn's 8 Best Success Lessons* (Issaquah, WA: Made for Success Publishing, 2014).

3. Cited in "Close Friends Less Common Today, Study Finds," Jeanna Bryner, Live Science, November 4, 2011, https://www.livescience.com/16879-close-friends-decrease-today.html.

4. Timothy Keller, sermon on "Friendship," May 29, 2005, YouTube video, uploaded by Gospel in Life, October 21, 2015, https://www.youtube.com/watch?v=8Tc4VIQrXdE.

5. Adapted from Janey Downshire and Naella Grew, *Teenagers Translated: A Parent's Survival Guide* (London: Vermilion, 2014), 14–17.

6. Quoted in Julia Scott, "Why is the Teenage Brain So Unpredictable? A Neurobiologist Explains," PBS, May 24, 2017, https://www.pbs.org/newshour/health/teenage-brain-unpredictable-neurobiologist-explains.

7. John Gottman and Nan Silver, *The Seven Principles for Making Marriage Work: A Practical Guide from the Country's Foremost Relationship Expert*, rev. ed. (New York: Harmony Books, 2015), 50–51.

8. Quoted in Alyson Weasley, "The Role of Friendship in Marriage," Focus on the Family, 2007, https://www.focusonthefamily.com/marriage/sex-and-intimacy/the-role-of-friendship-in-marriage/the-role-of-friendship-in-marriage-my-best-friend-my-spouse.

9. Les and Leslie Parrott, *Relationships*, 79.

Chapter 12

1. Quoted in Abby Jackson, "Tom Brady Used his Super Bowl Loss to Teach His Kids an Important Lesson About Failure," Business Insider, March 7, 2018, https://www.businessinsider.com/tom-brady-parenting-after-super-bowl-loss-2018-3.

2. Quoted in Jackson, "Tom Brady."

3. Deanna Conners, "Why Are These Biologists Dressed up as Whooping Cranes?" *EarthSky*, October 28, 2014, https://earthsky.org/earth/why-are-these-biologists-dressed-up-as-whooping-crane.

4. Nick Cady, "The Impact on Kids of Dad's Faith and Church Attendance," nwww.ickcady.org, June 20, 2016, https://nickcady.org/2016/06/20/the-impact-on-kids-of-dads-faith-and-church-attendance/.

Chapter 13

1. Dr. Emerson Eggerichs, "What Is Love and Respect?," Love and Respect (website home page), https://loveandrespect.com/.

2. "9th Inning," *Baseball*, first broadcast September 28, 1994 by PBS, directed by Ken Burns and written by Ken Burns and Geoffrey C. Ward.
3. Dr. Ross Campbell, *How to Really Love Your Child* (Colorado Springs: David C. Cook, 2015), 40.

Chapter 14
1. Charleen Alderfer, "Roots and Wings," PsychCentral, October 8, 2018, https://psychcentral.com/lib/roots-and-wings/.
2. "Individuation," GoodTherapy, last modified April 28, 2016, https://www.goodtherapy.org/learn-about-therapy/issues/individuation.
3. Zig Ziglar, *See You at the Top*, 2nd rev. ed. (Gretna, LA: Pelican Publishing, 2005), 317.
4. Dave Ramsey, "How to Teach Teenagers about Money," Dave Ramsey, https://www.daveramsey.com/blog/teach-teenagers-about-money.

Schedule Rodney Gage To Speak

Throughout his 30 years as a sought-after speaker, Rodney has been featured at some of America's largest churches, conferences and corporate events. He is also the author of seven books on parent-teen relationships. In addition, he has spoken to over 2 million students in public & private schools and has been featured on over 150 radio & television talk shows.

Family Shift Live Event

Help the families in your church, community or company "make the shift!" During this two-hour marriage & parenting event, Rodney & his wife Michelle will teach their proven 5-step framework that will strengthen and transform family relationships. This entertaining and highly engaging event will give families the insight and tools they need to start living with greater intention in their most important relationships.

Attendees will learn:
- How to agree on a desired destiny for their family and then create a plan to get there.
- Integrate family values and create a healthy culture in the home.
- How to deal with many common family issues before they become serious problems.
- How to make the shift from where they are to where they desire to be in their most important relationships.

▶ **For more information go to familyshift.com**

Follow Rodney & Michelle On Social Media

➤ **Rodney Gage**

𝐟 Facebook.com/Rodney.gage.3

⊙ Instagram:@rodneygage

🐦 Twitter:@rodneygage

➤ **Michelle Gage**

𝐟 Facebook.com/michelle.gage.9

⊙ Instagram:@michelle_gage

🐦 Twitter:@michellegage

➤ **Follow Family Shift on Social Media**

🌐 Web:Familyshift.com

⊙ Instagram:@familyshift

🐦 Twitter:@familyshift.com

𝐟 Facebook.com/familyshift

▶ YouTube.com/familyshift

FAMILY SHIFT
PODCAST
with **Rodney & Michelle**

The Family Shift Podcast with Rodney & Michelle Gage is a life-giving, podcast designed to give hope and how to's so you can shift your most important relationships from where you are to where you desire to be.

♫ **Listen on iTunes**

▶ **Watch on YouTube**

➤ **Familyshift.com/podcast**

VIRTUAL COACHING:
Transform Your Family Relationships In 31 Days!

Traditional marriage and family counseling can be too time consuming and expensive which is why we created a private digital coaching experience. Our 31-day online personal coaching experience is designed for couples/parents who want to turn their most important relationships around. In the privacy of your own home Rodney and Michelle Gage can personally walk you through specific ways on how you can make the necessary shifts to start living with greater intention in your marriage and family.

Here are 3 proven ways Rodney & Michelle can help.

- **Personal Coaching**
  You get to email Rodney personally so he can specifically address your situation and needs.

- **Live Coaching Calls**
  You get to talk directly with Rodney and Michelle through live phone or video conference calls where you and the other participants can ask them questions and get practical feedback.

- **Relationship Mentoring**
  Your participation in this digital coaching experience includes access to their online courses designed to serve as an on-going mentoring for your marriage and family relationships. Research shows that coaching/education is superior to traditional clinical counseling when it comes to achieving your greatest intentions.

➤ **Check out familyshift.com for more information.**

Other Books
By Rodney & Michelle Gage

RETHINK LIFE:
HOW TO BE DIFFERENT FROM THE NORM
Most of us approach life based upon childhood influences or what popular culture says is normal. When we understand the eternal purpose and role God has for our lives, it changes everything. In this book, authors Rodney and Michelle Gage will challenge you to reTHINK life from God's perspective by looking at seven key areas of life.

WE CAN WORK IT OUT: CREATIVE CONFLICT
RESOLUTION WITH YOUR TEEN
This book offers profound insights into the cause and effect of parent/teen conflict, as well as creative, Christ-centered approaches to effective conflict resolution. Find hope and encouragement for lasting change - peace and harmony - in any home.

WHY YOUR KIDS DO WHAT THEY DO:
UNDERSTANDING THE DRIVING FORCES BEHIND YOUR TEENS BEHAVIOR
A examination of the parent/teen relationship, this book teaches parents how to look beyond the often misleading symptoms of their child's negative behavior and address their true individual needs.

BECOMING THE PARENT YOUR TEENAGER
NEEDS
A 90 day devotional providing inspirations for daily encouragement. With Scriptural insight about God's will for each of us, this book will enrich and enlighten the "teen years" for every parent.

IF MY PARENTS KNEW...
DISCOVERING YOUR TEENAGER'S UNSPOKEN NEEDS
This book offers practical, common sense advice for parenting teenagers. Hear teenagers speak to you from their heart, in their own words, and from their own perspective of life. They share their hurts, their dreams, and their disappointments.

▶ **Purchase these books on Amazon.com**